A NEW MODERNITY?

WENDY WHEELER

A NEW MODERNITY?

Change in science, literature and politics

Wendy Wheeler

Lawrence & Wishart
LONDON

Lawrence & Wishart Limited
99a Wallis Road
London E9 5LN

First published 1999

British Library Cataloguing in Publication data.
A catalogue record for this book is available from the
British Library.

ISBN 0 85315 877 0

Typeset in North Wales by
Derek Doyle & Associates, Mold, Flintshire.
Printed and bound in Great Britain by
Redwood Books, Trowbridge.

Contents

To Bella, Ollie, Beattie and Tilly

I can see my fellow beings going down very gradually, and I call out
to them and explain: I can see you going down very gradually.
There is no reply. On distant charter cruises there are orchestras
playing feebly but gallantly. I deplore all this very much, I do not like
the way they all die, soaked to the skin in the drizzle, it is
a pity, I am severely tempted to wail. 'The Doomsday year,' I wail,
'Is not yet clear / so let's have / so let's have / another beer.'

But where have the dinosaurs gone? And where do all these sodden
trunks come from, thousands and thousands of them drifting by,
utterly empty and abandoned to the waves? I wail and swim.
Business, I wail, as usual, everything lurching, everything
under control, everything O.K., my fellow beings probably drowned
in the drizzle, a pity, never mind, I bewail them, so what?
Dimly, hard to say why, I continue to wail, and to swim.

Hans Magnus Enzenberger
The Sinking of the Titanic.

Acknowledgements

As always, one's indebtedness in the writing of a book must always go far wider than can actually be acknowledged. That said, I must firstly acknowledge permission to use material originally published elsewhere. Chapter 2 first appeared, in more limited form, in *New Formations* 3 (Summer, 1998). Parts of chapter 3 first appeared in *Literature and The Contemporary*, edited by Roger Luckhurst and Peter Marks (1999). I am grateful to Longman for permission to use this material. Parts of chapter 4 and chapter 5 appear in Geoff Andrews et al (eds) *New Left, New Right and Beyond: Taking the Sixties Seriously* (1999 forthcoming). My thanks to Macmillan for permission to use the material. Similarly, parts of chapter 4 will be found in Anne Coddington and Mark Perryman (eds), *The Moderniser's Dilemma* (Lawrence & Wishart, 1998). I am also very grateful to Graham Swift for generous permission to quote extensively from his novels. I am grateful to the University of North London for providing the sabbatical leave which allowed me to do the bulk of the research for the book, and for the on-going encouragement from colleagues there. Not least amongst these, a special mention must go to my office-mate, Paul McSorley, whose continual feigned surprise at seeing me at my desk at all served as a constant reminder of the extent of the University's support to me via relief from teaching. My publishers Lawrence & Wishart have been continually supportive, and I owe a particular debt, for meticulous reading, to Vicky Grut and Sally Davison.

On a more personal note, I am grateful to the Signs of the Times group, and its publications, for allowing me various opportunities to develop the ideas found here in their earlier formulations. Most of all I am grateful to many friends for endless hours of discussion and, in particular, to Carolyn Burdett and Jonathan Rutherford whose generosity – in giving their time to lengthy conversations, in reading parts of earlier versions of the manuscript, and in providing general encouragement, support and eating time when spirits flagged – was invaluable. To Steve Baker I owe several years of friendly encouragement and unflagging confidence; his own work, particularly in encouraging me to re-read Hélène Cixous, was a steady source of inspiration. Needless to say, all errors are mine alone, including, especially, the index which is just as orderly a list as you might expect from an author who doesn't get on very well with the shade of Jeremy Bentham.

Lastly, I owe a very special debt to my children Bella, Ollie, Beattie and Tilly, whose tolerance of maternal time – and attention-juggling, and doubtless deplorable other idiosyncrasies – has made the writing of this book possible.

London 1999

INTRODUCTION

The problem of reality

It is assumed here that the task of reality-acceptance is never completed, that no human being is free from the strain of relating inner and outer reality, and that relief from this strain is provided by an intermediate area of experience which is not challenged (arts, religion, etc.). This intermediate area is in direct continuity with the play area of the small child who is 'lost' in play.

Donald Winnicott[1]

If there's one thing that the world of modernity is centrally concerned with, it is reality. Thus, when we think about the eighteenth-century Enlightenment, we think about the attempt to grasp the real world as it really is – whether in the rise of the realist novel, in the realism of empirical method in the sciences, or in the determined realism of Utilitarian philosophy. The trouble is though, as Winnicott noted, that people are not very good at handling reality; or at least they need some relief from it. And the experience of modernity, for many people, is distressingly unrelenting: uncushioned, the demand to 'face the realities of the modern world' may become intolerable. We have, indeed, been freed in some senses: freed from the grip of tradition and superstition; freed from an all-encompassing religious intolerance; freed to say and do more or less what we want, and to make whatever we have the energy to make. But then there is, famously, the other side, in which we experience our freedom as also a kind of alienation and rootlessness. We are no longer restrained, but we are not held either.

A general sense of malaise hangs over Western culture. Although our lives are incomparably easier than any lived before, we recognise, amongst so much material comfort, a dreadful spiritual impoverishment. Our 'intermediate areas of experience which are not challenged' – that is to say, our *really* free and alive experiences of being what Winnicott liked to call a 'real person in the world' – are, in fact, increasingly invaded by what Carlyle contemptuously called 'the cash nexus' and its attendant managers.

So is it all up with us? Are we a civilisation in inevitable decline, to be replaced, as some think, by generations of cold and selfish warrior capitalists whom we would hardly recognise as human, and who rejoice in what Foucault once called 'the end of man' – or else by fundamentalist theocracies nostalgically seeking to restore certainty and faith? Or can the extraordinary adventure of human Enlightenment, with its high aims of rationality, freedom and progress for all humankind, find within itself a renewed understanding capable of a self-reflexive transformation? My argument in this book is that the resources exist for such a transformation, and that, at the end of the twentieth century, there is work being done in the fields of culture, science and philosophy which, taken together, represents the beginnings of a process of transformation which will enable us to imagine a new modernity.

THE POSTMODERN THORN

I often think that the further we move from Shakespeare in time, the closer we come to him in sensibility. I never can think about *Lear* without thinking of Beckett's *Endgame*; and Jacques Derrida's *Spectres of Marx: The State of the Debt, the Work of Mourning, and the New International*, which is a sustained meditation on living with ghosts, always brings to mind *Hamlet* – Hamlet's 'the time is out of joint' apparently applies to us too. Of course, things are always changing, but there do seem to be times when change is more intense and when time *has* got out of joint. That, I think, explains our affinity with the raging and betrayed Lear and with the prototypic modern melancholic Hamlet.

What historians now call the early modern period (of Shakespeare and the Renaissance) shares some of the features of the period which we have taken to calling postmodern, particularly in its 'big' questions about human meaning and significance. Both periods express the turmoil of uncertainties economic, social and spiritual. We can now see this historical turmoil as the foment of ideas from which the Enlightenment – and subsequently our own modernity – began to emerge in the last half of the seventeenth century. Can our postmodernity similarly be seen as the chaotic grounds from which a new modernity or second Enlightenment might emerge? Certainly both Jean-Francois Lyotard, and Zygmunt Bauman have argued that the postmodern is the necessary historical and conceptual *condition* of the modern.[2]

For Lyotard, the postmodern is like the crossing of the Alps in Wordsworth's *The Prelude*.[3] It is the sublime moment – unknowable and unrecognisable in itself – which can only be recognised retrospectively as the 'what will have been done'. For Bauman, 'modernity is postmodernity refusing to accept its own truth'[4]; this truth is that the aims of clear, ordered and systematic rationality were always an illusion. With the postmodern we once again begin to accept the mysteries of human impulses and are even suspicious of 'unemotional, calculating reason'.

The argument in this book – close in spirit to both Lyotard and Bauman – is that, in a sense, modernity comes too soon; or, at least, that its temporality is problematic. Bauman understands that the aim of 'disenchanting' the world had to be an illusion; postmodernity brings 're-enchantment' of the world 'after the protracted and earnest ... modern struggle to disenchant it'. As he adds, 'more exactly, the resistance to enchantment ... was all along the "postmodern thorn" in the body of modernity'. And Lyotard understands that the postmodern artist (or philosopher, or scientist) always 'comes too soon' to be understood. Leibniz, for example, makes a lot of sense once you have understood Darwin and Mendel. This problem with the temporality of modernity induces a condition of cultural 'melancholia', or 'failed mourning'. That is to say that modernity involves an encounter with loss – of the certainties of tradition and God – which is precipitous; it comes before the modern world has the conceptual tools for dealing with it. In other words, to mourn successfully means that you must be able to replace the complex affective world you have lost with a new, but equally human, complex affective world. Enlightenment modernity, with its commitment to reason, was a great leap forward; but its limited view of rationality meant that it could not offer a sufficiently wide and rich cosmology in place of what had been lost. The 'disenchanted' world of Enlightenment rationality was an impoverished one. My argument here is that we are now in a position to become truly modern: our science – especially our neuroscience and science of complexity – offers us a new cosmology of great subtlety and depth, in which our understandings of our human selves and our place within the world of culture and nature will be immeasurably enriched. This will constitute a proper mourning for the old world which Western cultures began to lose four centuries ago.

In this book I attempt to bring together work from different fields – critical and creative responses to the problems of Enlightenment modernity – in order to begin to articulate what might constitute the elements of a new modernity. In Chapter 1 I draw on the work of Raymond Williams in *Culture and Society*, and on Freud's *Civilization and Its Discontents*. In *Culture and Society* Williams traces the emergence of the modern idea of culture via 'cultural' responses to the experience of modernity; and, in *Civilisation and Its Discontents*, Freud traces psychical responses. My argument here is that Enlightenment modernity has involved 'rationalist' and 'individualist' responses which are characteristically toned by the psychical state of inner splitting and self-persecution which Freud describes as melancholia; I suggest that the Romantic stress on the virtues of human creativity, transcendence and love, and upon Coleridge's notion of art as producing 'unity from diversity', can be seen as an affirmation of the Freudian life drive (Eros) against the deathliness of disenchantment. Romanticism thus constitutes an attempt at cultural mourning – albeit a deeply problematic one. By setting Raymond Williams's *Culture and Society* beside Freud's *Civilisation and Its Discontents* I hope to persuade you of the claim that there is something of the death drive in the instrumentalism of modern rationalisations and bureaucratisations. Particularly where these latter are in the service of capitalist profit to the exclusion of all other human goods, the effects upon human beings are likely to be dehumanising and deathly.

In Chapter 2, I take another look at the possible effects of Enlightenment ideas of rationality. Once more looking at modernity's tendency to bring about dualistic, or split, thinking, I concentrate this time on the 'major' psychical splitting associated with psychosis and, in particular, on the emergence of so-called 'borderline' personalities in the twentieth century. I refer to evidence (both medical and cultural) which suggests that borderline psychosis has been on the increase for a number of decades; and I suggest that this may be the result of Enlightenment's gendered organisation of identifications, in relation to rationality and irrationality, with men identifying with a form of reason which is organisationally powerful but affectively impoverished. One way of expressing this might be to say that by the beginning of the nineteenth century, power resided with Adam Smith's analysis of political economy in *The Wealth of*

Nations, while his *Theory of the Moral Sentiments* lay forgotten.

In Chapter 3, I offer a literary case study of the work of the English novelist Graham Swift. Swift's work exemplifies the artistic struggle with Romanticism as a problematic solution to the most disturbing aspects of modernity. This is followed by a more general consideration of creative disorderliness as an aspect of mourning-work.

Chapter 4 offers an examination of managerialism as a characteristic modern response to ethical relativism, and considers the contemporary rise of managerialism in a post-ideological politics. I argue that politics cannot be simply about management but must always involve choices – which are, in fact, always about what is good and what is bad. I also argue that current cultural and scientific developments and changes (to be discussed in more detail in Chapter 5) require a political response.

In Chapter 5, I detail shifts in sensibility across a range of fields in which the distinct spheres of knowledge articulated in Enlightenment philosophy seem to be breaking down and in flux. I suggest that this signals the possibility of a new modernity, a form of healthy cultural mourning at last, and show how these changes are to be found at the heart of the contemporary sciences of complexity and neurobiology.

In conclusion I note that the cartesian dualism which has so fundamentally structured the modern world is in the process of being replaced by what is, in the broadest possible sense, an ecological sensibility. In this, certain kinds of distinctions – mind/body, reason/passion, and perhaps other cognate ones – seem to be giving way to a more holistic way of thinking. Our modern senses of such things as order, reason, body, and so on are being greatly and usefully expanded through a growing understanding of the creative complexity of the world, and of the creatures amongst whom we move and in whom we have our being – as do they in us.

NOTES

1. D. Winnicott, *Playing and Reality*, Routledge, London 1991, p13.
2. J-F. Lyotard, 'Answering the Question: What is Postmodernism?', in Lyotard, *The Postmodern Condition: A report on Knowledge*, [1979], tr. G. Bennington, E B. Massumi, Manchester University Press, Manchester 1984.
3. In *The Prelude*, the poet and his companion crossing the Alps ask a local

peasant for the right path to the summit of the pass. The peasant tells them that they have already crossed the summit of the pass.

4. Z. Bauman, *Postmodern Ethics*, Blackwell, Oxford 1993, p32.

CHAPTER 1

Modernity
Reason and progress

Terms such as modernity, romanticism, and postmodernity are always imprecise; their value is heuristic, inasmuch as they allow us to refer to our sense that, at some very approximate period in time, important changes occurred in the ways in which people understood both themselves and the time of which they were a part. In this book the word modernity refers, roughly, to a period of two hundred or so years, from the mid to late eighteenth century up to the mid to late twentieth century. My use of the term romanticism will, I hope, shortly become evident. By postmodernity I mean the period during which certainties – especially about the value of science, rationality, and progress – began to be called into question. It is quite clear to me that the Nazi Holocaust and, perhaps to a lesser extent, the use of atomic weapons against Japan at the end of the Second World War, played a very significant part in the development of a postmodern sensibility. As is always the case, however, that sensibility developed and was elaborated over time: its early manifestations appeared in the 1960s, but were not widespread until the 1970s.

The purpose of this chapter is, first, to offer a sketch of the philosophical and intellectual conditions from within which the tensions of modernity – which I am shortly to describe in a particular way – developed. Inevitably perhaps, the philosophical seeds of modernity – particularly in the work of Leibniz, which I discuss briefly below – contain the potential resolution of the conflict of ideas which have characterised this two-hundred year period. Profoundly embedded conflicts of ideas always take a long time to work themselves out; it is nevertheless surprising, given that the modern age has been, above all, a scientific age, that only fairly recently has the scientific Zeitgeist become sufficiently attuned to the times to produce research capable of bringing a scientific underpinning to ideas produced in the late seventeenth and early eighteenth centuries when the spirit of modernity was just getting underway.

The chapter's second aim is to identify significant pieces of work from two modern thinkers – Sigmund Freud's *Civilisation and its Discontents* and Raymond Williams's *Culture and Society* – which can usefully be read through each other in order to provide a theoretical basis for thinking about the animating spirit of modernity, and beyond that a way of thinking about the significance of cultural symptomatologies at the postmodern end of the twentieth century.

What I will argue throughout both chapter and book is that modernity is characterised by an essentially melancholic response to the loss of traditional beliefs, and that postmodernity is the coda to modernity inasmuch as it restages cultural grieving in all its potential aspects, but at a new level of intensity – both in punitive melancholic modes and also, latterly, in tentative attempts at wholesome mourning. Thus, the initial cultural symptoms of postmodernity were a nostalgic attempt – sometimes ironic or parodic, for instance in architecture – to refuse modernism's futurism and to hold on to the past,[1] and theoretical languages which were punitive in their view of human beings, as fragmented and decentred, and were couched in a prose designed to punish its readers. The second stage of postmodernism, I will argue, is oriented towards the future, towards ways of rethinking human beings as whole souls in a newly-conceived world, and towards a 'postmodern' rebuilding which might constitute a true mourning of what was lost in the first modernity. In this second stage of postmodernity, we may be able to find ways of thinking about the world which are sufficient to allow us to make a new kind of modernity from the wreckage of the first.

LOOKING AT THE FIRST MODERNITY

By the middle of the eighteenth century, the aim of philosophy – that is to say science – had fundamentally changed. In the seventeenth century, the application of reason was viewed within the contemplative model as the process of logical and clear thought whereby, at best, one might arrive at and participate in a truth already and divinely in eternal existence. By the middle of the eighteenth century, reason was no longer conceived in this context but, rather, in terms of movement or change – to know something more or new. From this time on, it is in the very movement of the mind itself that reason is expressed as critical thought: 'Diderot, himself originator of the *Encyclopaedia*, states that its purpose is not only to supply a certain body of knowledge but also to bring about a change in the mode of thinking – *pour changer la façon commune de penser*. Consciousness of this task affects all the minds of the age and gives rise to a new sense of inner tension. Even the calmest and most discreet thinkers, the real "scientists", are swayed by this movement'.[2]

In other words, as a revolution in scientific thought, Enlightenment modernity must be understood to be something profoundly *unbinding*; it releases movement from the stilling constraints of tradition, belief and contemplative knowledge and into the forward flow of analytic thought fed by, and always starting from, the endless facts of the physical universe. Science as exemplified by the methodological approach of Newton, in which one proceeds from facts in the material world to a theoretical explanation, rather than from a point of theoretical or metaphysical clarity to the meaning of things in the world, parts company with art; and thus philosophy, particularly as an empirical science, is poised to become the new truth-language of modernity. With the formulation of the new discipline of aesthetics in the mid-eighteenth century art increasingly takes up the language of moral sensibility which once belonged to religion.

Here, we can see the beginning of the separation of areas of knowledge which, towards the end of the eighteenth century, Kant will inscribe in his three Critiques of Pure Reason, Practical Reason and Judgement. In spite of the clarity of analytical thought that this development will allow, it is this separation which will, eventually, lead to the anxiety – characteristic of modernity and described in Raymond Williams's *Culture and Society* – that utilitarian philosophy leads to a dehumanising of the life-world.

At the beginning of the eighteenth century the idea of moral virtue is gradually becoming separated from a religious sensibility, and, by the middle of the century, aesthetic appreciation will, in its turn, begin to define a distinct sphere in which sensitivity to works of art invokes a state of mind akin to virtue. We can trace these movements of Enlightenment thought in the work of Shaftesbury, Adam Smith and Baumgarten. By the century's end, scientific philosophy, in the shape of Benthamite utilitarianism, will thus offer a very different kind of knowledge about the world to that found in art. In the form of Romanticism, the latter will still retain, in vestigial form, its long association with religion. As the nineteenth century progresses, Romantic thought and practice will find itself increasingly opposed to the instrumentalism of utilitarian modernisation.

Lord Shaftesbury's *An Inquiry Concerning Virtue, or Merit*, for example, written during the last quarter of the seventeenth century, argues that true virtue derives from the human possession of a moral sense, rather than merely from religious fear of punishment or hope of reward. Its conclusion, that true virtue lies in an apprehension of God's perfection and in a desire to do justice to this in the world as well as in one's own person, rather than in religious dread, is thus theistic.[3] On the question of why people should be virtuous in the wider sense of caring for the good of the whole rather than simply attending to private virtue, Shaftesbury argues that the pursuit of pleasure will lead us to the maximal pleasure of social love. Adam Smith's *Theory of the Moral Sentiments* takes up similar questions and is at pains to base moral sentiment in a sensibility born out of affective identification. Smith's economic theory, as propounded in *The Wealth of Nations*, assumes moral social empathies and cohesion as the necessary basis for the pursuit of individual profit in free markets. These moral grounds, based upon the articulation of bourgeois inwardness in terms of fine feelings and (middle-class) identifications, are the 'taken for granted' of the cultures in which the doctrines of political economy, utilitarianism and *laissez-faire* are developed. As many critics have noticed, this brings about both an aestheticisation of the moral self and also the feminisation of morality, famously typified by the nineteenth-century idealisation of the woman as 'the angel in the house'. The latter is the gentle she whose domestic spirit provides the protected 'home' from which the entrepreneurial male, replenished, daily sets forth to parry and thrust in the competitive market place. As Terry Eagleton argues, 'The ultimate binding force of the bourgeois social order, in contrast to the coercive apparatus of absolutism, will be habits, pieties, sentiments and affections'.[4] With this, he adds, power has become aestheticised as Baumgarten's '"sister" of logic, a kind of *ratio inferior* or feminine analogue at the lower level of sensational life'.[5]

I shall return to the question of gender, and the gendering of ideas, later. For the moment, I simply want to note that one of the most striking things about social and political debate at the end of the 1980s and during the 1990s was an increasingly clear recognition that the combination of scientific rationality as the truth-language of modernity, and the steady development of individualism since the sixteenth century, has tended to erode the shared system of social and moral values upon which the development and success of capitalist societies depend. John Gray's analysis in *Enlightenment's Wake*, for example, makes just such an argument, as does Paul Ormerod's *The Death of Economics*.[6] It is also no coincidence that these current anxieties about a weakening of moral sense – which have been expressed both generally in Western societies, and, specifically, in Britain during the neo-liberal Conservative governments of sleaze and greed between 1992 and 1997, are also expressed in anxieties about family breakdown and 'problems' in terms of gender identifications. Without anyone quite saying it, what causes anxiety – about education, families, proper aesthetic education and taste (leading, in 1998, to a call for Civic Studies to be compulsorily taught in schools) – is the middle-class fear that all the ingredients necessary to the bourgeois soul are no longer being provided in society. Capitalist commodification, and the growth of a middle class now raised on mass culture, raise the spectre of a dystopic future in which depthless and amoral individuals consume and litigate their way through a world governed by global markets.

LOOKING AT SEEDS

The sense that there is something injurious to the social whole in modernity, and that there is something problematic about the analytic, dissecting and calculating mathematical spirit of Enlightenment science, has, however, a much longer history than its most recent expressions in the 1990s. It is this history which Raymond Williams describes in his 1958 book *Culture and Society*.

Before turning to Williams's account, I think it is worth looking at Ernst Cassirer's work, the philosophical sources of the apparent opposition between the individual and the whole, or between an individualist, atomising and mechanistic view (essentially utilitarianism), and the organicist view associated with Romanticism. These views are significantly represented in the philosophy of Leibniz, which came to the attention of Enlightenment thinkers, largely via Wolff, with the posthumous publication of Leibniz's *New Essays on the Human Understanding* in 1765 (Leibniz died in 1716). Through Wolff's pupil Alexander Baumgarten, Leibniz's work was influential in the development of German aesthetic theory (which would eventually become Romanticism), but in France its effects were felt most in the philosophy of nature, where 'Leibniz's conception of evolution now receives more and more stress ... it gradually transforms, from within, the eighteenth-century system of nature which had been dominated by the idea of fixed species'.[7]

Briefly, for Leibniz, creation is made up of individual entities or monads which are dynamic and evolving, but there is a relationship between each individual monad and the universe which is indissoluble. It is not simply that each monad is essentially a part of the universe, but that each individual part or fragment expresses the whole universe from a particular viewpoint. As Cassirer says:

> ... in Leibniz's philosophy an inalienable prerogative is first gained for the individual entity. The individual no longer functions merely as a special case, as an example; it now expresses something essential in itself and valuable through itself. For in Leibniz's system every individual substance is not only a fragment of the universe, it is the universe itself seen from a particular viewpoint. And only the totality of these unique points of view gives us the truth of reality.[8]

As Cassirer goes on to point out, Leibniz's philosophy draws the individualism of the cartesian *cogito* together with a sense of the relatedness of life, into a dynamic holistic evolving system. But while these ideas of organicism form the basis of German and English Romanticism, the dominant scientific temper of the nineteenth century seems to have been more attracted to the ideas of origins and development, which Leibniz's dynamic monadology also described.

It is very easy to see why a conserving attitude will grow so readily into a Romantic one during the nineteenth century; and it is equally easy to see how German Romanticism, popularised in England largely by Coleridge, will be able to argue that the genius of the romantic artist lies in his ability to express the symbolic unity of the universe, in spite of all its apparent diversity, through his work. This view accords with the individualism of the age which is otherwise expressed in the utilitarian philosophy of self-interest.

Leibniz's philosophy is not only helpful in understanding the philosophical sources of the tension between individual and social whole; it is also a quite extraordinary forerunner not only of nineteenth-century evolutionary thinking but, more importantly, of the evolutionary neurobiology developed in the past few years, a point I shall return to in chapter 5. What is remarkable about Leibniz is that, like Darwin and Freud after him, he had a grasp of a theory without having the science necessary to elaborate his intuition fully. His was an evolutionary theory of the embodied and enworlded mind, which would be capable of overcoming the dualism which was one of Enlightenment's most fatal bequests to modernity.

Throughout the nineteenth century these two accounts of the significance of the individual will, as Williams shows, struggle and contend, and the conflict is still very much alive in the twentieth century. This tension in responses to Enlightenment modernity – between, on the one hand, a reforming utilitarian philosophy, informed by a cartesian sense of the individual as agent in a mechanical and manipulable world, which would be so successfully deployed by industrial capitalism, and, on the other hand, a socially conserving romanticism – is precisely the tension described by Raymond Williams in *Culture and Society*. In everything which follows, I will aim to show how, in art, in science and in politics, the tension within the mathematical spirit of Enlightenment is expressed in the conflict between scientific reason – which develops both the calculations of utilitarianism *and* evolutionary theory – and an aestheticised reason (by no means always politically unproblematic), which eventually expresses itself, from the 1960s onwards, in (Leibnizian) terms in which the old opposition begins, at last, to break down. This is most notably the case in the development of ecological science, but it is evident in other scientific and cultural spheres also. I will be arguing that this breaking down of the older dialectical oppositions is something akin to a form of mourning, or to the regaining of the ability to hold binding and unbinding elements together (the form of mourning which Melanie Klein describes as the 'depressive' position).[9] But first, Raymond Williams.

RAYMOND WILLIAMS, THE FIRST NEW LEFT, AND *CULTURE AND SOCIETY*

Before looking in more detail at *Culture and Society* I think it is important to establish the context in which the work was written and to say something about Williams's own intellectual place and time. His effort formed a part of the enterprise of the first New Left, a loose grouping of intellectuals towards the end of the 1950s, whose work attempted to mount a critique of both advanced consumerist capitalism, and of the reformist version of socialism pursued by the British Labour Party within the postwar consensus, an approach which they viewed as being too wedded to an outmoded understanding of class, and too committed to Labourism, managerialism, and centralised economic control.

The first New Left, with which Williams is associated, and within which his was an influential voice, was formed loosely from two sources: on the one hand the provincial Northern English group, including E.P. Thompson and John Saville, who produced, first, the journal *The Reasoner* and, after their exit from the Communist Party of Great Britain, *The New Reasoner*; on the other hand the Oxford and then London based, more cosmopolitan, group which produced the *Universities and Left Review*. Prominent members of this latter grouping included Raymond Williams, Stuart Hall, Raphael Samuel and assorted critics and artists such as Doris Lessing, John Osborne and Trevor Griffiths. In 1959 the two journals merged to form the *New Left Review*.[10]

Although this first formation of the New Left only lasted until 1961, when *New Left Review's* first editor Stuart Hall was replaced by Perry Anderson, the effects of Williams's and Hall's interventions in terms of widening the conception of the proper object for socialist thinking were immense. It was they who insisted that the growth of postwar capitalism and the development of a mass consumerism – G.K. Galbraith's 'affluent society' – should be seen as forming a cultural totality, and that mass forms of culture such as advertising and television are as worthy of study as 'high' art, if not more so for what they can tell us about the society we live in. Thompson was resistant to this emphasis on culture, preferring a more rigorously economic and historical analysis. Williams and Hall were convinced that unless the British Labour Party could understand the depths of the social changes occurring during the postwar period, and take proper cognisance of the need for a political response to these changes, it would remain incapable of adapting and changing and, above all, incapable of providing a distinctively socialist response. In the view of some, this failure to think and thus to respond to what was happening economically and culturally in the late 1950s vacated the intellectual ground upon which, in the 1970s, the New Right would sow its ferocious seed.

The New Left, and the early *New Left Review*, had identified themselves aesthetically with modernism, especially in its critique of representation and language as transparent,[11] and socially with modernisation. As Michael Kenny points out, for some New Left critics, especially Raphael Samuel writing in 1989, 'the empathy with modernity provides the key to understanding much of the New Left's political identity: its modernistic zeal was potentially elitist and Fabian in inspiration, anticipating the culture of expert planning which came to dominate social provision in the 1960s'.[12] Samuel refers to the argument made in the first issue of *Universities and Left Review* by the architect Graeme Shankland, in which the latter claimed that slum clearance could only succeed if undertaken in 'a great combined operation and under a single directive intelligence [which would] ... prevent what he called the "monotony of muddle"'.[13]

Here, for me, there is a significant echo with Stephen Blackpool's 'aw a muddle' in Dickens's *Hard Times*. In the novel the 'muddle' is associated negatively with the reluctant strike-breaker Blackpool, but positively with Sissy Jupe and the circus from which she hails; the circus stands as a romantic resistance to the intellectual utilitarianism of Thomas Gradgrind and, more especially, to the industrial capitalist utilitarianism of Josiah Bounderby. Mud, muddle and circuses recur in *Hard Times* as images of the good soul at work in the world, and of a certain kind of grace which modernity cannot allow. When, after her disastrous love-less marriage to Bounderby, and her near seduction by the affectless James Harthouse, Louisa Gradgrind returns, splattered in the mud of a storm, to her father's house, she cries out to her uncomprehending parent: 'Father ... How could you give me life, and take from me all the inappreciable things that raise it from the state of conscious death? Where are the graces of my soul? Where are the sentiments of my heart?'[14]

This, written in 1854, expresses the essence of Romanticism's struggle against the controlling and 'deathly' utilitarian father-figure who is so much *the* archetypal figure of nineteenth-century culture (more of which in the next chapter). It also expresses something of the revulsion against control, and the 'single directive intelligence' which Samuel retrospectively voices in regard to earlier New Left commitments to modernisation. Of New Left attachments to reformist zeal, Samuel remembers:

> In housing and town planning we stood for comprehensive redevelopment, advocating 'islands of compact buildings' or 'towns within cities' as an alternative to subtopia and sprawl. Vallingby, Stockholm, was one of our models, 'the new attractive LCC flats at Roehampton' another – high-rise blocks on a site 'formerly ... wasted by crumbling, decaying and totally uneconomic Victorian mansions' ... We also presented ourselves ...as avatars of the motorcar age, praising, in *ULR* 2, the 'great sculptural beauty' of the new Los Angeles flyovers and attacking the British road system as 'archaic' ...[15]

The tone of the above quote needs no comment. What is significant is the folly which Samuel, in 1989, associates with the modernist idea that 'a single directive intelligence', bent on eradicating muddle and messiness in the name of a sweeping utopian landscape and future, could hope to maintain anything of a human-ness which, as Freud points out in *Civilization and Its Discontents*, is notably characterised by messiness, disorder and decay over time.[16]

Here, in Samuel's implicit distrust of the drive to bring order too quickly, in the valuing of past forms of the urban landscape, and in the suggestion that modernity does something ruthless and destructive (that is to say 'hard') to human time, it is possible to see the outlines of that turn to the past, and revaluing of an organic 'messiness', which forms a part of the postmodern sensibility. At the end of the 1950s, both Irving Howe and Harry Levin used the term 'postmodernism' to indicate a malefic condition of mass culture: 'Harry Levin used the ... concept of the postmodern to designate what he saw as an "anti-intellectual undercurrent" which threatened the humanism and enlightenment so characteristic of the culture of modernism'.[17]

By the late 1980s, and writing in a way which might very readily be identified with a 'deplorable' postmodernist nostalgia, Raphael Samuel speaks a quite different sensibility in relation to broad cultural inclinations. By the late 1980s, 'postmodernism' still means mass culture, but the nostalgic symptomatologies of the latter are treated with less contempt by intellectuals and artists.[18] Indeed, and as in Samuel's own 1994 work *Theatres of Memory* (1994), virtues as well as vices are found in the mass consumption of history produced by the so-called 'heritage industry'. Literary postmodernism in the 1980s and 1990s is distinguished by a similarly critical disinterring of history.[19]

All this is possible because of a widely experienced sense that aesthetic modernism, and cultural modernity, are sometimes brutal and brutalising; and because of the sense – acutely felt in the post-war period after the experience of nazism – that forms of rationality which exclude feeling and popular sentiment (good or bad) as forms of knowledge, as *active* (good or bad) common sense, can lead to something inhuman in one way or another. Feeling may be dangerous, but from the 1980s onwards there is increasingly a gradual sense that the graces or disgraces of the soul need to be entered into the account.

It is possible, then, to say that, both in Britain and the United States, similar New Left concerns were expressed about inadequate left responses to mass consumer culture and advanced commodity capitalism – Galbraith's culture of private wealth and public squalor: there were anxieties about the disruption of communal ties (evidenced not least in the sense of the alienation and disaffection of working-class youth, which was exemplified by Teddy Boys on the streets, and in film by Marlon Brando's role in *The Wild Ones* and James Dean's in *Rebel Without A Cause*) and in the loss of earlier class identifications.

Nevertheless, certainly where the British left were concerned, no great contradiction was seen between a recognition that the successes of capitalism, with its great emphasis on individualism, tended to fragment communities and identities, and a continued commitment to utilitarian approaches to reforming order, as described by Samuel in his 1989 remembrance.

The seeds of recognition are certainly present – most strongly in Williams's *Culture and* Society- but they need recasting in a slightly different language, in order to show how the change from Raphael Samuel's modernism in 1959 to his postmodernism thirty years later could come about without any true inconsistency.

THE HISTORICAL 'MOMENT' OF *CULTURE AND SOCIETY*

What I have said so far constitutes, then, the historical and conceptual context of *Culture and Society*, in which Williams discovers a history of modernity in the dialectical antagonism between utilitarianism, reform and modernisation on the one hand, and romanticism, conservatism, organicism and connectedness on the other. Psychoanalytically inclined critics, and those disinclined to accept linear temporalities, might want to say that rather than 'discovering' a history at this crucial moment of cultural anxiety in the late 1950s, Williams retrospectively *reconstructs* the past in a form that helps to make sense of the present experience of crisis. Historiography is always about construction and reconstruction, and no connotation of 'falsification' should be attached to what Williams does here. It is always only in the present, and because of the present, that we find ourselves obliged to re-understand and re-order the past. Psychoanalysis, too, itself, is always rightly self-implicated in the dialectics of reconstruction and deconstruction; but this hardly matters: we are always *producing* the history and the narratives which will allow us to make a new sense of what has happened to us. This is normal.

For Freud, this act of *Nachträglichkeit* (usually translated as 'deferred action', and meaning the very real ways in which memorial reconstruction alters our *present* self-understandings and *present* real experience[20]) would be a fundamental gesture in a psychical mechanism of memory which must construct its own past in this way. This is not as outlandish as it might at first appear. In particular it is a characteristic response when 'something has gone wrong'; it is a response to trauma in other words. The first response to something shocking, destabilising and threatening is to try to construct a narrative which will make sense of it. All of us will be aware how, under such conditions, we are often obliged to 'read' the past differently. Commonly, in this situation, one finds oneself obliged, under the pressure of events, to reinterpret as *significant* an event or events which *apparently* had no particular significance at the time. Of course, this rather begs the question as to why apparently insignificant events have been remembered at all,[21] and what it is about such events that allows us retrospectively to invest them with a meaning which they did not *appear* to carry at the time. But, nevertheless, this *is* how contemporary events sometimes bear in upon us; and in this way we are obliged to tell a different history.[22]

History and time – which has become something more complex than the mere telling of beads on a string – are characteristically postmodern concerns, whether this is expressed in the strange histories and temporalities of contemporary novels, or simply in the way that Bauman and Lyotard are able to say that the postmodern is the very condition of the modern.[23] Here the postmodern anxiety – a brush with a sublimely (that is to say traumatically) unbinding apprehension – produces the narrative which will make sense of present terror (and hide, or bind up its awfulness) by retelling history in such a way as to accommodate it.

In the 1950s, Williams 'discovers' a history of modernity in nineteenth-century critiques of industrial capitalism, which he himself then describes in the 1982 'New Foreword' to *Culture and Society* as returning to 'make startling connections' with the 'new ecological and radical-ecological' movements of the late 1970s and early 1980s. Noting that *Culture and Society* had, in the past, been 'confidently analysed, and in some cases dismissed, as the merely romantic critique of industrialism or industrial capitalism', Williams's 'New Foreword' makes the point that these nineteenth-century anxieties have not gone away.[24] While many have tried to keep faith with the idea of social and scientific progress, many have also found, in the dilemma described in *Culture and Society*, the continuing kernel of a problematic modernity which remains our problem still. The history of ideas which Williams uncovered still provides a way of orientating oneself politically in regard to debates about the virtues of modernity and modernisation at the very end of the twentieth century. Indeed, this, as much as the uncovering of history, was how Williams himself regarded the work. It is clear from Williams's 1982 'New Foreword' that, for him, *Culture and Society* was not *just* a history, but was a history *as work*:

> But I did not write it only as a history ... I began it in the post-1945 crisis of belief and affiliation. I used all the work for it as a way of finding a position for which I could hope to understand and act in contemporary society, necessarily through its history, which had delivered this strange, unsettling and exciting, world to us. It may not work in that way for others, but that is why it was written and how, by more readers than I had hoped for, it has often been read.[25]

In those 'voices which came through' from the past, as fellow strugglers in our present, we can hear quite clearly what sort of a work the book is. The language is the language of mediumship, the voices those of the unquiet dead who haunt us still, and the book – taken forward by the present 'into dimensions which are much more than repetitive' – an attempted act of mourning which might provide rest for these uncanny, and uncannily prescient, eighteenth- and nineteenth-century ghosts who speak in it.

In order to show more precisely how this is so, and to translate Williams's historical 'structures of feeling' into a more detailed language of affect and unconscious drives which might be capable of illuminating modernity and postmodernity also, I must now turn to Freud.

CIVILIZATION AND ITS DISCONTENTS

In a sense *Civilisation and its Discontents*, written in 1929 (Freud's suggestion for the English title was 'Man's Discomfort in Civilization'), is the culmination and cultural application of all Freud's metapsychology. In it one can see, for example, the effects of Freud's 'Mourning and Melancholia', written in 1915, where the idea of the super-ego (not named there as such) began to be explored. In 'Mourning and Melancholia' Freud developed the idea that a part of the ego takes the form of its ideal (a figure of authority and power, usually a father-figure, which Freud called the 'ego-ideal'), which splits off from the ego and stands in perpetual judgement upon it. This idea is clarified in *The Ego and the Id* (1923) where the term superego is introduced. In *Civilization and its Discontents*, the superego, and its role as the relentless voice of self-criticism, is the internalised agency of the demands of civilisation in which outward expressions of aggression must be relinquished. Although the guilt and aggression to which the superego gives voice are largely unconscious, its effects are, Freud noted, very similar to the inner voice of conscience; with it, aggressivity is directed inwards towards the ego.

In 'Mourning and Melancholia', Freud's view is that aggression is directed towards the self because the relation to the source of loss or betrayal (whether a person or an idea) is narcissistic: that is to say there is an overidentification with the lost loved thing, which is 'saved' from final departure by being psychically introjected. Thus, punishment truly intended for the lost person or cause is directed towards the self with which the lost thing is intimately identified. This narcissistic element in superegoic self-punishment does not, however, appear very fully in *Civilization and its Discontents*.

In 'Mourning and Melancholia', the Freudian melancholic is a *failed* mourner. That is to say, he or she has never successfully negotiated the ending of a narcissistic relation to the mother. In his discussion of the psychical structure of the modern subject in *Civilization and its Discontents*, Freud knows that the superego is the internalised voice of cultural authority which gains some narcissistic pleasure from 'control over nature',[26] but the question of narcissism and of narcissistic relations to objects (whether people or ideas) – so prominent in the essay on melancholia – is not satisfactorily addressed in terms of investments in cultural forms. Indeed, in a footnote added in 1931, Freud refers to this 'gap' in the account.[27]

I think the reason for this 'gap' can be found in Freud's emphasis on the superego as the voice of the 'father', combined with his reluctance to think about the persistence of narcissistic feelings in relation to the mother and, more widely, in relation to cultural forms which could be said to be forms of the mother. Because of this, and because of a general lack of interest in what mothers do, Freud is unable or unwilling to think about the significance of the mother, or of cultural forms of her, in the relinquishment of narcissistic identifications. This means that he is unable to think about whether or not modern civilised selves are, generally speaking, successful or failed mourners (in my view the implication of his essay is that they are melancholics); nor is he able to think about the cultural forms – forms of symbolic mothering – which allow narcissism to end, or at least to be diffused across cultural life, and which thus work to mitigate the effects of the superego. In fact, Freud explicitly passes over mothering both at the beginning and at the height of the argument he develops in *Civilization and its Discontents*. I will return to this later.

In *Civilization and its Discontents* it is also possible to see the influence of Freud's work in *Beyond the Pleasure Principle* (1920). In this work Freud pursued the significance of 'the compulsion to repeat' and arrived at the conclusion that his earlier formulations of the drives (ego and sexual) needed to be replaced by an idea of the life drives (or 'Eros, the preserver of all things'[28] – a wider conception than simply sexual) and the death drive. In *Civilization and its Discontents*, as in 'Mourning and Melancholia', the death drive is linked to the problem of aggressivity and its internalisation by the punishing superego; but this time it is as a consequence of civilisation rather than simply the narcissistic response to loss. As I implied above, this broadening of the scope of this argument begs the question of whether there is something increasingly and narrowly narcissistic about the 'modern' post-Reformation self, particularly as it emerges in its increasingly secularised form in the nineteenth and, more strongly, twentieth centuries. Christopher Lasch has remarked upon the dangers of a 'culture of narcissism' in the twentieth century, and has noted how this has manifested in an increase in the symptomatologies associated with 'borderline', or near-psychotic, affective disturbance.[29] Once again, I will come back to this question about the ways in which outwardly non-brutal cultures symbolise affection and connectedness later.

The 'compulsion to repeat' returns also in the 1930 work, where it is identified as the drive at work in the modern desire for 'cleanliness and order': 'Order is a kind of compulsion to repeat which, when a regulation has been laid down once and for all, decides when, where and how a thing shall be done, so that in every similar circumstance one is spared hesitation and indecision. The benefits of order are incontestable'.[30] This, itself, is related back to the aggressivity of the anal/sadistic phase in which anal control (and the correct secreting away of deposits of various kinds) is accomplished. Knowing, as we do now, the compulsive ordering and docketing bureaucracy of the Final Solution, we might be less willing to agree with Freud about the 'incontestable benefits' of order; but this is something which I will discuss in Chapter 2 where I look at possible reasons for the post-modern 'crisis' of reason in Western societies.

Finally, both 'Mourning and Melancholia' and *Beyond the Pleasure Principle* take their points of departure from considerations of experiences of traumatic loss in which the normal dominance of the pleasure principle in psychical life is brought under the sway of the death drive implemented by a persecuting superego. In *Civilization and its Discontents*, this sadistic and demanding inner voice of 'conscience' is specifically identified as the 'discomfort' of modernity.

THE COSTS OF CIVILISATION

The essence of *Civilization and its Discontents* is Freud's belief that civilised societies demand an internalisation of aggressive instincts which, in earlier pre-modern societies, had been allowed a fuller external expression. For Freud, aggressivity is a more primitive emotion than the socially binding instincts which, here, bear the name of Eros. The *final* aim of the aggressive instinct is, says Freud, that of returning the organism to an earlier condition of absolute order in which there is no disturbance at all – i.e. death. Where Eros (the life drives) works to bond together more and more individuals (or individual organisms) into complex collective forms, the death drive seeks to unbind, to separate and, ultimately, to end life. In its aim-inhibited form its tendency is to seek mastery and control. Its libidinal expression is, of course, sadism. For Freud, it is as if Eros is a sort of late colourful diversion in which the aim of preserving life is, simply, that, on the long road to death, each thing should die only the death which is immanent in it rather than any other: 'What we are left with is the fact that the organism wishes to die only in its own fashion', says Freud.[31]

Thus, Freud will say in *Civilization and its Discontents*:

> And now, I think, the meaning of the evolution of civilization is no longer obscure to us. It must present the struggle between Eros and Death, between the instinct of life and the instinct of destruction, as it works itself out in the human species. This struggle is what all life essentially consists of, and the evolution of civilization may therefore be simply described as the struggle for life of the human species. And

it is this battle of the giants that our nurse-maids try to appease with their lullaby about heaven.[32]

The enchantments offered by women caring for small children are treated, here, with the scorn which such illusions deserve; but, as with the matters of love, loss, narcissism and culture referred to above, I shall also want to return to uncanny enchantments later – particularly as these are described, by Donald Winnicott, in terms of 'transitional' spaces and objects. Winnicott's transitional spaces are quintessentially *creative* spaces, and I will have reason to return to them, and their avatars, again and again in what follows.

Freud's concern in the essay on civilisation is that the internalisation of aggressivity (in the form of the superego) would eventually prove intolerable. In other words, he asks if the costs of civilisation actually involve an intensification of deathliness (hatred, unbinding, atomisation and alienation) which will spell an end to the Enlightenment dream of progress.

Freud's discussion in the essay involves a lengthy investigation of aggressivity, guilt, and the formation and activities of the superego. From this Freud derives his central thesis that modern civilisation – it would be easier just to say nineteenth-century modernity – produces guilt (in the form of internalised and self-directed aggressivity) in a more or less exponential form which Freud thinks might become unbearable:

> If civilization is a necessary course of development from the family to humanity as a whole, then – as a result of the inborn conflict rising from ambivalence, of the eternal struggle between the trends of love and death – there is inextricably bound up with it an increase of the sense of guilt, which will perhaps reach heights that the individual finds hard to tolerate.[33]

In other words, the demands of modern life are that aggressivity must be internalised and put to productive use in the form of orderly work in the world. But, for Freud, however internalised aggressivity might be, it still produces guilt. Nothing can hide one's aggression from the all-seeing paternal or God-like internal eye of the super-ego; thus, with every aggressive thought, the individual feels ever more guilt.

As societies become outwardly less brutal, they set up the internalised structures of the superego more firmly, and this leads to a racking-up of the death drive in the form of unconscious aggressivity and guilt. Where belief systems can encompass this, and provide a means of offering escape from aggressivity and guilt and a reaffirmation of love (or Eros in the now wider sense), the racking-up may remain bearable because symbolisations and rituals of atonement and cleansing are available for dispersing it. Christianity offers, at least in its Catholic form in which absolution is available via the priest, a striking example of such a system. But where no such externally mediated forms of absolution are to be found, where one confronts only the merciless voice of a conscience which sees every wriggle of the guilty worm's aggression and further guilt, the melancholic structure of self-punishment becomes increasingly lethal. Where love fails, or where – to use Julia Kristeva's formulation – there is 'no space for love',[34] the great force of the self-punishing death drive may be turned, catastrophically, against the ego itself. If modernity cannot find spaces for love, or its disorderly, creative avatars, its suicidal or para-suicidal tendencies may, on a mass cultural scale, become overwhelming. In this context, Theodor Adorno's assertion, written in 1946/7 with a clear glance towards the rational utility of the Nazi death-camps, that 'the task of art today is to bring chaos into order' is entirely comprehensible.[35]

THE PROTESTANT WORK ETHIC

Before coming to a conclusion about how *Civilization and its Discontents* can be read in such a way as to throw a different light on the oppositions of *Culture and Society*, it may be helpful to turn briefly to another text altogether. Readers familiar with Max Weber's *The Protestant Ethic and the Spirit of Capitalism* (1904-5) will have no difficulty in recognising Freud's essay as a sort of psychoanalytic elaboration of the theological shifts which Weber describes as making capitalist modernity possible. Indeed, Freud comes very close to Weber at points, both in the discussion of religion's use of the 'sense of guilt' in the form of conscience,[36] and in the passages concerned with 'the cultural superego' (of which Luther and Calvin are fine examples) and ethics,[37] and also in his remarks concerning socialist insights into the erosion of a society's ethical life through too much emphasis on the importance of possessions.[38]

The Protestant Ethic and the Spirit of Capitalism describes the progress of modern, capitalist societies as deriving from the religious changes of the Reformation in the sixteenth century. For Weber, modern societies, and the work ethic which motivates them, depend upon the shift from the Catholic idea of God as external to the self, in which one's sins are confessed to the priest who acts, via the Church, as a mediator between God and the individual, to the Protestant idea of a direct and unmediated relationship between God and person. In this relationship, the individual's faith is not so much in the Church, but in the direct revelation of the presence of God to the individual, whose conscience becomes, so to speak, the voice of God within. In other words, in Protestantism, the voice of God is revealed in individual faith, and the commands of God are thus acted out by the individual in his own life. The proof of faith is no longer in the hands of the priest, but in the hands of the individual who shows his good faith in his life-work – his work in the world – as a 'calling'.

With this shift, the Protestant ethic of the manifestation of God's grace by good works in the world is born. Where religious asceticism came out of the monasteries and, with the Reformation, entered everyday life,[39] the ascetic self-mastery of the medieval monk entered the mundane world of virtuous bourgeois life. Weber refers to Sebastian Francks' observation that the significance of the Reformation was 'that now every Christian had to be a monk all his life'.[40]

As with Freud's anxiety about the intolerable and deathly effects of modernity, Weber, too, wonders whether the secularisation of religious asceticism in the form of modern utilitarianism will not lead to a deathly 'nullity'. His conclusion is that what began as the idea of work in the world as a religious calling, with success in it being the possible mark of grace and of membership of God's Elect, has ended in the calling to the 'iron cage' of capitalist production – the work of an internalised God as conscience and conscientiousness. So although Weber writes that 'when asceticism was carried out of monastic cells into everyday life, and began to dominate worldly morality, it did its part in building the tremendous cosmos of the modern economic order', he also comments that 'no-one knows who will live in this cage in the future ... For of the last stage of this cultural development, it might well be truly said: "Specialists without spirit, sensualists without heart; this nullity imagines that it has attained a level of civilization never before achieved"' (pp181-2).

Freud's not dissimilar anxiety – and it is equally, in some sense, an anxiety about the failure of 'spirit', 'heart', and 'love' (Eros) – is expressed in the idea that too much harshness (especially internalised and self-directed), too much demand for the order and perfection of the, now secular, 'calling' to bourgeois success, and too little ability to find something lifeful – that is creative, non-calculable, even disorderly or chaotic – to counteract it, will end in the triumph of precisely something deathly like Weber's 'nullity'.

What Williams discovers in *Culture and Society* is that the dialectic of modernity involves a tension between, on the one hand, the utilitarian impulse to rational order and reform based on the claims of the rights of the individual, and, on the other hand, the romantic impulse to affirm the social and collective nature of human beings. In other words, *Culture and Society* is precisely a sustained historical exploration of that struggle described by Freud as the struggle between Eros and Death. In it, scientific, technological, social and political progress seem, at the same time, to tear up by the roots tried and tested (albeit 'unfair' by modern standards) ways of living and relating in the world. Whether one is inclined to call these 'costs' of modernity spiritual or psychical hardly matters: costs they are; and from them flow the very many concerns with the idea of 'community' which, fractiously, arise in the late 1950s, and keep recurring into the 1970s, 1980s and 1990s. Contemporary anxieties about the possibility of community – and their expression in ideas (which are really ideals) of a community of women, or a 'black' or a 'gay' community – all attest to the fact that community, in the sense of humans living together and relating in the world, has become a marker of something lost (and therefore something to be mourned and repaired) in postmodern society.

Within the writings of the eighteenth and nineteenth centuries, the idea of culture gradually shifted from being about the cultivation of land to being about the cultivation of people. Thus, for Wordsworth, culture was 'the embodied spirit of a People'; and this – the 'embodied spirit'- was positioned as the mightiest weapon in the battle against philistine capitalists. As Williams writes: 'Culture, the "embodied spirit of a People", the true standard of excellence, became available, in the progress of the century, as the court of appeal in which real values were determined, usually in opposition to the "factitious" values thrown up by the market and similar operations of society'.[41]

What, in Freud's essay, is the great battle between 'Eros, the preserver of all things', and source of the impulse to bind individuals into society with one another, and Death, whose work is competition, aggressivity and the unbinding and atomising of groups and selves, appears in *Culture and Society* as the struggle between 'romanticism' and utilitarian capitalism.

For us, this latter is so 'naturalised', so associated with the Establishment and with political Conservatism, that is easy to forget that, in the first half of the nineteenth century, capitalism – to both owners and industrial workers alike – was widely seen as potentially socially destabilising. On the evidence of Elizabeth Gaskell's *North and South*, for example, both the new breed of uncultivated, *nouveaux riches*, 'sprung from nothing' capitalist entrepreneurs, *and* the anonymous workers which their mills drew into the new northern cities, represented a form of new and potentially threatening energy. Mrs Gaskell makes much of the spirited independence of both workers (including young women) and bosses, which she contrasts with the social conservatism of the southern elites and dull-wittedness of their rural labourers. In *North and South* (1854-5), both mill-owner John Thornton *and* his striking workers are identified with imagery which is terrifying and sublime. Thornton is a sort of industrial version of *Jane Eyre*'s Mr Rochester, dark, Byronic and uncultivated – at least in the eyes of the southerner Margaret Hale – while the demonstrating workers are represented with all the fascination and terror of the sublime:

> The women gathered round the windows, fascinated to look on the scene which terrified them ... Mrs Thornton watched for her son, who was still in the mill ... Then he called to the women to come down and undo his own door ... And the sound of his well-known and commanding voice seemed to have been like the taste of blood to the infuriated multitude outside. Hitherto they had been voiceless, wordless, needing all their breath for their hard labouring efforts to break down the gates. But now, hearing him speak inside, they set up such a fierce unearthly groan, that even Mrs Thornton was white with fear ... As soon as they saw Mr Thornton, they set up a yell – to call it not human is nothing – it was as the demoniac desire of some terrible wild beast for the food that is withheld from his ravening.[42]

Margaret Hale, daughter of a southern rural clergyman newly moved to a northern industrial city, represents taste, gentility and the civilising effects of beauty, love and the connectedness of the old rural ways. It is concern for the decline of these, which mean the decline of traditional forms of relationship, which unites the otherwise enormously different Edmund Burke and William Cobbett – the 'contrasts' with which Williams opens *Culture and Society*. Similar in his opposition to the sublimely unbinding forces of industrial capitalism, Wordsworth elevates poetic beauty and the special task of the poet in these terms: 'He is the rock of defence for human nature; an upholder and preserver, carrying everywhere with him relationship and love'.[43] In other words, Eros is art, love and binding-up; utilitarian capitalism is the sublime work of the death drive unleashed.

The late eighteenth-century interest in the uncanny and the sublime – as evidenced in Gothic literature and painterly representations of sublime imagery – has been described, precisely, as a massive cultural unleashing of uncanniness (i.e. deathliness). Mladen Dolar, for example, argues that 'there is a specific dimension of the uncanny that emerges with modernity', and suggests that what had once been socially and psychically contained within the realm of the sacred flies loose in frightening ways in secularising societies. Noting the ways in which popular culture gives expression to these changes in the form of gothic fiction and art, Dolar argues that the explosion of ghosts, vampires and undead (and, for the first time, flying fairies) in the 1790s is 'something brought about by modernity itself'.[44]

Reading Williams back through Freud and Weber produces a powerful sense, confirmable in other sources such as Baudelaire, that bourgeois utilitarian modernity is experienced as both radical and death-driven. As Foucault reminds us, Baudelaire's painter of modern life is:

> the one who can show the dark frock-coat as 'the necessary costume of our time', the one who knows how to make manifest, in the fashion of the day, the essential, permanent, obsessive relation that our age entertains with death. 'The dress-coat and frock-coat not only possess their political beauty, which is an expression of universal equality, but also their poetic beauty, which is an expression of the public soul – an immense cortège of undertaker's mutes (mutes in love, political mutes, bourgeois mutes ...). We are each of us celebrating some funeral'.[45]

Thus, the experience of modernity induces cultural melancholia – a ceaseless condition of a mourning which does not know how to end: a *failed* mourning. I have also suggested that postmodernity is a condition (not to be confused with its symptomatologies in cultural life – many of which are, themselves, profoundly melancholic: both fragmented and manic) which involves the attempt to move from a failed mourning to a successful one.

MOTHERS AND FATHERS – A PRELUDE

Thus far, I have suggested that we might usefully think of modernity as caught up in a new, poorly culturally symbolised struggle between the Life and Death drives which Freud identifies in *Civilization and its Discontents*, and which Williams finds in Romanticism's Leibnizian *connectedness* of individual 'points of view of the universe' in the form of collective resistances to utilitarian liberal individualism. What both texts allow us to see is the emergence of a series of homologous oppositions – science/art; reason/passion; mind/body; individualism/collectivism – which most readers will have no trouble recognising as culturally gendered.

I shall develop an argument concerning this more fully in the next chapter; for the moment I want to conclude here by noting how Freud approaches the whole argument of *Civilization and its Discontents* via a lengthy refutation of motherliness as a source, or mediation, of religious experience. Later psychoanalytic theorists of the sources of symbolic life have sought precisely a return to the transitional function of the mother as symbolic mediator of the violences of the castrating paternal injunction 'Thou Shalt Not!'. But first, let us turn to the opening of *Civilization and its Discontents* in order to see Freud begin the marginalisation of femininity in relation to cultural life and its transmission.

The actual source and starting pointing for *Civilization and its Discontents* was a letter from Freud's friend Romain Rolland. This letter was sent to Freud in response to Rolland's reading of Freud's essay on religious beliefs: 'The Future of an Illusion' (1927). Freud reports that, in his letter, Rolland:

> was sorry that I had not properly appreciated the true source of religious sentiments. This, he says, consists in a peculiar feeling, which he himself is never without, which he finds confirmed by many others, and which he may suppose is present in millions of people. It is a feeling which he would like to call a sensation of 'eternity', a feeling as of something limitless, unbounded – as it were, 'oceanic'. This feeling, he adds, is a purely subjective fact, not an article of faith; it brings with it no assurance of personal immortality, but it is the source of the religious energy which is seized upon by the various Churches and religious systems, directed by them into particular channels, and doubtless also exhausted by them. One may, he thinks, rightly call

oneself religious on the ground of this oceanic feeling alone, even if one rejects every belief and every illusion.[46]

Finding no such sentiment in himself, Freud's response is to offer a psychoanalytic account. This is that, in spite of our sense of unity and autonomy, the ego is not so sharply defined, that it continues 'inward' into the unconscious and – in at least one state which we would not call pathological – outward so that the boundary between self and other is, indeed, blurred: 'At the height of being in love the boundary between ego and object threatens to melt away. Against all the evidence of his senses, a man who is in love declares that "I" and "you" are one, and is prepared to behave as if it were a fact'.[47] Further: 'An infant at the breast does not yet distinguish his ego from the external world as the source of the sensations flowing in on him'.[48]

There follows a relatively lengthy discussion of the persistence of archaic forms, and Freud concedes that the 'oceanic' feeling described by Rolland can doubtless be traced back to an earlier phase of 'ego-feeling'. But Freud will not have it that this can be the source of religious feeling because 'a feeling can only be a source of energy if it is itself the expression of a strong need'.[49] And for Freud, there is no need in childhood which is 'as strong as the need for a father's protection'.[50] Thus, the source of religious feeling lies in the exaltation of the figure of the father derived from the child's helplessness:

> Thus the part played by the oceanic feeling, which might seek something like the restoration of limitless narcissism, is ousted from a place in the foreground. The origin of the religious attitude can be traced back in clear outlines as far as the feeling of infantile helplessness. There may be something further behind that, but for the present it is wrapped in obscurity.[51]

This is, one might think, a strange move. But it is characteristic of the Freudian focus on the patriarch. The more obvious deduction, from almost everything Freud says until the point at which he declares that Rolland's 'claim does not seem compelling',[52] is that the 'oceanic feeling' of limitless narcissism and love, and the experience of pre-oedipal oneness at the mother's breast, suggest that the source of religious feeling does, indeed, lie with the limitless narcissism associated with the pre-oedipal relation to the mother.

Now, Freud's view of aggression is dependent upon an absolute separation of love and hate: even where, as in sexual encounters, they appear to work together, in general they oppose each other entirely. Aggression is, in a sense, the prior, or more fundamental, emotion since it is this which drives the Freudian fantasy of the primal horde and the murder of the father which liberates the circulation of women and forms the basis of the social group and 'love'.[53]

In this anthropological fantasy, the sons love the father, but they hate him first. Freud posits this as, perhaps, the originary guilt (born of ambivalence) from which all further guilts may follow. For Freud, aggression and Eros can only work together in an essentially sadistic form whereby mastery is directed outwards to the world, in the form of mastery of the other, so that the organism diverts the primal urge to self-destruction. In *Civilization and its Discontents* Freud sees the religious commandment to 'love thy neighbour' as an injunction arising from the actual fact that aggression is the primary motive amongst men, and that they are generally relentlessly hostile to each other in one way or another. Love, in this view, is a way of binding together groups *after* a primal aggression, and it is *opposed* to that death-driven aggression. It is this which allows Freud claim that even though it is women, through the circulation of Eros, who 'found' civilisation, they are generally hostile to its 'modern' forms on the ground that its demands, for the internalisation of aggression and sublimation of erotic drives, force them 'into the background'.[54]

But there is another way of looking at love which does not give primacy to aggression, but which places love and aggression as drives which must be reconciled. With Melanie Klein, the language of psychoanalysis works towards an account in which the maternal relation forms the basis of a (rather fragile) reconciliation of the drives which Klein called the 'depressive position'. In this, a primitive tendency to splitting the psychical world into good and bad objects (good breast and bad breast) is overcome in a process of mourning, by the achievement of a psychical state in which good and bad, hate and love are tolerated together.

In the post-World War Two period, and symptomatically I would say, because at the time the need to find a way of reconciling apparently oppositional forces had become very urgent, D.W. Winnicott began to formulate a theory of aggressive mastery which did not focus upon the father's sadistic castrating command at all. Instead, it focussed upon a form of command – to come into being, to desire, and to renounce limitless narcissism – which was articulated by the mother.

In this chapter I hope I have shown how Williams and Freud can be read through each other in order to produce an understanding of modernity's experience of loss, and will to remake through reform, as unbinding, death-driven, and melancholic. In this reading, romanticism presents itself as a problematic will to life (and mourning) which is, nonetheless, still caught in a dialectic of 'splitting'. In other words, if utilitarian philosophy founds itself upon a limited view of rationality as empirical realism, romanticism, equally, founds itself upon a transcendent understanding of human beings in the world which supposes that 'spirit' and 'art' are inexplicably 'other-worldly'. Neither is adequate and, in this, Dickens's view of Sleary's slightly subversive human circus as a form of opposition to utility arguably offers a better symbol. At least the circus is firmly grounded in the mess and muddle of truly human creativity.

In the next chapter, I will argue in more detail about the nature of the splitting at the heart of the project of modernity, and look at some of the ways in which this is played out in terms of gender.

NOTES

1. C. Jencks, *What Is Postmodernism?*, Academy Editions, London 1986.
2. E. Cassirer, *The Philosophy of Enlightenment*, tr. F.C.A. Koelln & J.P. Pettegrove, Princeton University Press, Princeton, New Jersey 1968, p14.
3. Lord Shaftesbury, *An Inquiry Concerning Virtue, or Merit* (1714), D.Walford (ed), Manchester University Press, Manchester 1977.
4. T. Eagleton, *The Ideology of the Aesthetic*, Blackwell, Oxford 1990, p20.
5. *Ibid.*, p16.
6. J. Gray, *Enlightenment's Wake: Politics and Culture at the Close of the Modern Age*, Routledge, London 1995; P. Ormerod, *The Death of Economics*, Faber & Faber, London 1994.
7. Cassirer, 1968, *op. cit.*, p34.
8. *Ibid.*, pp32-3.
9. See M. Klein, 'Mourning and Its Relation to Manic-Depressive States', in J. Mitchell (ed), *The Selected Melanie Klein*, Penguin, Harmondsworth 1986.
10. For a detailed history of the first New Left, see M. Kenny, *The First New Left: British Intellectuals After Stalin*, Lawrence & Wishart, London 1995.
11. *Ibid.*, p102.
12. *Ibid.*, p108.
13. *Ibid.*

14. C. Dickens, *Hard Times* (1854), Penguin, Harmondsworth 1985, p239.
15. Kenny, 1995, *op. cit.*, p109.
16. S. Freud, *Civilization and its Discontents*, Pelican Freud Library 12, Penguin, Harmondsworth 1985, p282.
17. A. Huyssen, *After the Great Divide: Modernism, Mass Culture, Postmodernism*, Indiana University Press., Bloomington & Indiana 1986, p161.
18. W. Wheeler, 'Nostalgia isn't Nasty: the Postmodernizing of Parliamentary Democracy', M. Perryman (ed), *Altered States: Postmodernism, Politics, Culture*, Lawrence & Wishart, London 1994.
19. This theme is too extensive to catalogue, but see, as an example, L. Hutcheon, 'Beginning to theorise postmodernism', *Textual Practice*, 1, 1, (Spring, 1987), which is also, slightly altered, a chapter in her *A Poetics of Postmodernism: History, Theory, Fiction*, Routledge, London 1988.
20. Neurobiologist Gerald Edelman, whose work I discuss in chapter 5, describes this kind of mental activity in terms of neural re-entry, i.e. the ways in which experience (including the re-organisations of remembered things) can act as feedback which alters the ways in which we 'map' the world in the present. G. Edelman, *Bright Air, Brilliant Fire: On the Matter of the Mind*, Penguin, Harmondsworth 1994.
21. Freud's conception of screen memories begins to address this question. S. Freud, Ch IV 'Childhood Memories and Screen Memories', in *The Psychopathology of Everyday Life*, PFL5, Penguin, Harmondsworth 1975.
22. For Walter Benjamin, such an interpretative ability, in which one is able to seize history by understanding the relation between apparently unrelated events across time, is the mark of the true historical materialist. In Thesis XVIII of the 'Theses on the Philosophy of History' Benjamin writes: 'Historicism contents itself with establishing a causal connection between various moments in history. But no fact that is a cause is for that very reason historical. It becomes historical posthumously, as it were, through events that may be separated from it by thousands of years. A historian who takes this as his point of departure stops telling the sequence of events like the beads of a rosary. Instead he grasps the constellation which his own era has formed with a definite earlier one. Thus he establishes a conception of the present as the "time of the now" which is shot through with chips of messianic time'. W. Benjamin, 'Theses on the Philosophy of History', *Illuminations*, H. Arendt (ed), tr. H. Zohn, Schocken Books, New York 1969.
23. J.F. Lyotard, 'Answering the Question: What is Postmodernism?', appendix to J.F. Lyotard, *The Postmodern Condition: A Report on Knowledge* (1979), tr. G. Bennington & B. Massumi, Manchester University Press,

Manchester 1984; Z. Bauman, *Postmodern Ethics*, Blackwell, Oxford 1993.

24. R. Williams, 'New Foreword' (1982) to *Culture and Society: Coleridge to Orwell*, The Hogarth Press, London 1987 (Chatto & Windus, 1958).

25. *Ibid.*

26. S. Freud, *Civilization and its Discontents*, PFL12, Penguin, Harmondsworth 1985, p313.

27. *Ibid.*, p273 n1.

28. S. Freud, *Beyond the Pleasure Principle*, PFL11, Penguin, Harmondsworth 1984, p325.

29. C. Lasch, *The Culture of Narcissism*, W.W. Norton & Co., London 1991 (1979). See especially Ch 2 'The Narcissistic Personality of Our Time'.

30. Freud, 1985, *op. cit.*, p282.

31. Freud, 1984, *op. cit.*, p312.

32. Freud, 1985, *op. cit.*, p314.

33. *Ibid.*, p326.

34. J. Kristeva, *Tales of Love*, tr. Leon. S. Roudiez, Columbia University Press, New York 1987, p61.

35. T. Adorno, '*In Nuce*', *Minima Moralia: Reflections from Damaged Life*, tr. E.F.N. Jephcott, Verso, London 1974, p222.

36. Freud, 1985, *op. cit.*, p329.

37. *Ibid.*, pp335-6.

38. *Ibid.*, p338.

39. M. Weber, *The Protestant Ethic and the Spirit of Capitalism*, Routledge, London 1992 (1904-5), p121.

40. *Ibid.*

41. Williams, 1987, *op. cit.*, p34.

42. E. Gaskell, *North and South*, Penguin, Harmondsworth, 1970 (1854-5), pp229, 232.

43. Williams, 1987, *op. cit.*, p41.

44. M. Dolar, '"I Shall Be with You on Your Wedding-Night": Lacan and the Uncanny', *October*, 58, Fall, 1991, p7.

45. M. Foucault, 'What Is Enlightenment?', in P. Rabinow (ed), *The Foucault Reader*, Penguin, Harmondsworth 1986, p40.

46. Freud, 1985, *op. cit.*, pp251-2.

47. *Ibid.*, p253.

48. *Ibid.*, p254.

49. *Ibid.*, pp259-60.

50. *Ibid.*, p260.

51. *Ibid.*, p261.

52. *Ibid.*, p259.

53. S. Freud, *Totem and Taboo*, PFL13. The matter of the primal horde, and

of the sons' ambivalence towards the father whom they kill, also recurs in *Civilization and its Discontents*, p325.

54. Freud, 1985, p293.

CHAPTER 2

In the middle

A third way with gender and other important ways of thinking about ourselves?

I don't see you as a *father* you know ... More a sort of *male mother* ...'

He disliked the term 'male mother' ... He distrusted the implication that nurturing, even when done by a man, remains female, as if the ability were in some way borrowed, or even stolen, from women – a sort of moral equivalent of the *couvade*. If that were true, then there was really very little hope.

Pat Barker, *Regeneration*[1]

INTRODUCTION: THE FATHER AND THE LAW

At the end of *My Own Private Germany: Daniel Paul Schreber's Secret History of Modernity*, Eric Santner describes Schreber as a writer whose *Memoirs* are the literalisation of the 'secret' of modernity.[2] And this secret is both the totalitarian fantasy of the completely penetrated and managed life-world and, concomitantly, the *failure* of Enlightenment modernity as autonomy lived in the real ordinary world.

The case of Judge Daniel Paul Schreber and the suffering he endured in childhood at the hands of his over-intrusive father has been well-documented,[3] but Santner's fascinating contribution is to link Schreber's experiences at the hands of his father to a wider crisis in what might be termed the symbolic function of the father more generally. Santner argues that Schreber's illness was precipitated by a 'crisis of investiture': when called to represent the law in the superior office of *Senatspräsident* from October 1893, Schreber – whose early personal experiences of the practical effects of the Enlightened father had been traumatic and maddening – was unable to go through with the ceremony.

The delusional system that Schreber developed in response to this crisis, Santner argues, was a distorted form of his recognition of something rotten in Enlightenment modernity. This rotten-ness, which had literally been inscribed upon his body in childhood by his father's system of 'rational mental and physical training', was expressed in Schreber's belief that, amongst other things, his body was putrescent and that he was being turned into a woman. Eventually, Schreber was able to turn this latter delusion into the psychotic's typical attempt at 'self cure'. He convinced himself that, while largely unpleasant, his being turned into a woman was of general benefit since he would eventually be able to bear a new race of children who would save the world. Was the madman imagining a female father?

Whatever the case, Schreber seems to be an embodiment of late modernity's sense of a crisis in the symbolic function of the father. In this chapter I intend to explore this sense of crisis more widely. In doing so, my aim is to draw attention to the highly gendered nature of modernity's structures of power, and to look towards a 'third way' for symbolic power, which might be able to exist 'in the middle of real things'.

SCHREBER'S RESPONSE TO DISCIPLINARY POWER

Santner compares Schreber's mythic version of modernity – which he describes as 'the institutional domain in crisis' – with Wagner's last opera *Parsifal*;[4] he notes that, where Wagner's mythic modernity finds the source of this 'chronic malfunction' in Kundry – woman and wandering Jew – and its healing in the memory of Amfortas's suffering and Kundry's death, the Schreberian theology resists such obvious 'otherings'. For Santner – or perhaps one should say for Schreber – the truth about modernity is to be found within the paternal law itself, and in what it does to its loyal sons:

> One of the many reasons for Schreber's appeal – for his remarkable 'attractiveness', as he would put it – and his belated canonization as a compelling modernist writer, is that he offers the prospect of new strategies of sapping the force of social fantasies that might otherwise lend support to the totalitarian temptation.[5]

Santner argues that Schreber's response to his personal crisis has a revelatory force (and that this ability to communicate may have helped him):

What ultimately saved Schreber from psychological death, at least for a short while, was no doubt his residual need and capacity to *communicate and transfer* his 'discoveries', to inaugurate a new *tradition* constructed out of and upon the inconsistencies and impasses of the one he had known and which he had been called upon to represent. (The proliferation of books, articles, conferences, and seminars dedicated to Schreber, which shows no signs of abating, testifies to the revelatory force and productivity of his transmission.)[6]

Using Foucault's distinction between juridical power and disciplinary power, in which the latter undermines the former, Santner argues that Schreber's delusional structure – his theology of the two gods in which one is properly distant, the other obscenely close and invasive – literalises the problem of power, authority and the law in Enlightenment modernity. The gods are also, of course, Schreber's own 'split' father, who exemplified Enlightenment pedagogy and methods of right training to a chilling, and sickening, degree.

Schreber's *Memoirs* are an illumination of the obscenely interfering nature of disciplinary power. His crisis is a response to the perverse interestedness at the heart of a (paternal) law which should be benignly disinterested. This too-interested disciplining leads to the break-down of any reverence for authority, and hence undermines that authority's ability to legitimate social structures – and thus the individuals who exist within them. How can one trust in the benign (because ultimately disinterested) authority of a father who is much too interested in – indeed libidinally fascinated by – the disciplining of one's own most intimate bodily details and functions, as was Schreber's father?

Schreber's over-interested and invasive father produced one son who was a suicide and another who became psychotic (and suicide is, Benjamin says, the other honourable response to modernity[7]). This tells us, of course, about another secret of modernity: rather than the neurotic, its model subject is either the self-persecuting melancholic or the persecuted psychotic; these are structurally similar creatures – the minor and major keys of psychical splitting.

As Santner argues, an individual's identity in the community is formed through procedures of symbolic investiture – through the performative power vested in the state, of rituals of naming and placing. This can be understood at its most formal level in terms of the offices of state; less formally, but still importantly, in the powers of investiture granted to institutions; and at its least formal (but not informal) in social institutions. The psychological health of a society's members, as well as its own social and political stability, appears to be correlated to the efficacy of these symbolic operations – 'to what we might call their *performative magic* – whereby individuals "become who they are", assume the social essence assigned to them by way of names, titles, degrees, posts, honours, and the like ... We cross the threshold of modernity when the attenuation of these performatively effectuated social bonds becomes chronic, when they are no longer capable of seizing the subject in his or her self-understanding.' In the case of Schreber, the threshold of his breakdown was the investiture ceremony. For Santner, the analysis of paranoia offers the insight that an 'investiture crisis' has the potential to generate not only feelings of extreme alienation, anomie, and profound emptiness – 'anxieties associated with absence'; it can also generate anxieties associated with overproximity:

> one of the central theoretical lessons of the Schreber case is precisely that a generalized attenuation of symbolic power and authority can be experienced as the collapse of social space and the rites of institution into the most intimate core of one's being. The feelings generated thereby are ... anxieties not of absence and loss but of overproximity, loss of distance to some obscene and malevolent presence that appears to have a direct hold on one's inner parts.[8]

This 'lack of the lack', an experience of a lack of distance from something obscene, malevolent or sublime, is precisely how Mladen Dolar, with reference to the theme of the 'split' father, also describes the experience of Enlightenment.[9] As a symbol of the law, and its ability to grant more or less stable identities and meanings, the father of modernity becomes deeply fractured. In regard to this splitting, Santner goes on to note arguments made by Foucault and Borch-Jacobsen. Foucault's 'Schreberian point' is that Enlightenment produces two modes of power, in which *disciplinary* power undermines *juridical* power and fosters chronic dysfunction; Mikkel Borch-Jacobsen's contribution to an understanding of the splitting of paternal law is his argument that the *complex* (as opposed to elementary) kinship structures of modern societies are accompanied by a 'narcissistic bastardization' of the paternal figure, in which the law of the father precisely no longer applies *as law*; hence, Santner argues, 'the modern dissolution of what Foucault refers to as "deployment of alliance" [which is the function of juridical power] almost necessarily produces men like Schreber'.[10]

THE 'AS-IF' PERSONALITY

As with so much of what is now referred to as the postmodern, the roots of this contemporary, late modern, interest in the significance of psychotic splitting as the 'secret' of modernity (as opposed to the diagnosis of modern melancholia with which we are familiar from Baudelaire to Benjamin, Adorno and Kristeva) can perhaps be found in the political experience of fascism in the 1920s, 1930s and 1940s. And one of the direct effects of the experience of fascism, arguably, was the beginning of the theorisation of a form of borderline personality (the borderline lies between sanity and madness) which, in 1942, Hélène Deutsch called the 'as if' personality.[11] (This form of borderline personality was first given wide popular cultural expression in the US in the 1950s in the form of what has been called 'social science fiction'[12]) The 'as if' personality appears sane 'on the outside', as it were, but (eventually, or under certain circumstances) reveals the inner affective deadness, or inauthenticity, of the psychotic. In 'as if's, psychosis is hidden.

One can have no trouble in seeing that totalitarianism, and the authoritarian father figures it produces, required some explanation. After the war, and especially during the 1950s when the full extent of totalitarian inhumanity perpetrated by apparently normal human beings became increasingly common knowledge, the category of the 'as if' personality – or, in *Invasion of the Body Snatchers* imagery, 'pod people' – must have seemed to offer something like the beginning of an answer. During this same period, psychoanalysis – particularly in the work of Donald Winnicott – also began the significant post-war turn away from the domestic primacy of the strong father and towards the importance of the role of the mother.

As with nineteenth-century resistances to utilitarian modernity, in which certain aspects of medieval life (the monastic community, for example, or the Gothic mason) were felt to embody forms of non-alienated experience, this maternal turn was also medieval in aspect, since it intended to return early childcare to women in a way that had not been orthodox since before the Humanism of the fifteenth century. It is crucial to know, however, that for Winnicott – and this is most clearly evident in his essay 'The Location of Cultural

Experience' – the mother becomes more of a mother/father or, in a version of Pat Barker's term, a 'male mother'.[13] For me, the question now is whether modernity's troubled father can make a similar move, but in ways which are *not* simply those of the *couvade*. This would imply a relinquishment of mastery in favour of something different – perhaps what Winnicott calls 'holding'. Without such a change, Barker is right to say that there really is 'very little hope'.

Psychoanalysis began to try to explain how apparently ordinary or normal people could behave 'psychotically' to other human beings – i.e. without a normal affective relatedness, as in Levinas's morality of the 'face to face'. This led analysts to pay attention to apparently normal individuals whose pathologies exhibited such fearfully deadened features. By the 1950s, 'as if'-ness – or 'False Self' organisation, as Winnicott termed it – was identified with the experience of *damaged* mothering. This post-war turn to the importance of the mother, and to what 'ordinary devoted mothers' spontaneously do when nothing gets in their way, was explicitly linked to the preservation of democratic societies. I shall return to this question of the symbolic and actual role of fathers and mothers later.

In the remainder of this chapter I hope to achieve a number of things. Firstly, I want to discuss Santner's *My Own Private Germany* in some more detail, in order to show how he links the failure of symbolic power to an excess of the disciplinary paternal law, which proceeds from Enlightenment but actually undermines its symbolic juridical function. In deploying this argument, I aim to show how the gesture of self-undermining, which has already been encountered as a striking feature of the progress of modernity, can be tied to the figure of a psychotically split father who stands for a disturbed symbolic world or 'law'. My argument is that this figuration does not arise out of a void, but is a representation of modernity's inculcation (Foucault would say 'disciplining') of bourgeois masculine virtues.

Secondly, I aim to show that a significant part of this failure of symbolic power results from an evacuation of symbolic forms of maternity from our culture, and from the acting-out of a masculine fantasy of replacing the mother, which is particularly associated with the subject of Enlightenment (Mary Shelley's *Frankenstein* is probably its first striking fictional representation).

Thirdly, I want to look at the rise of the category of the 'borderline' psychotic or 'as if' personality described by Hélène Deutsch, and to argue that this offers a disturbing model of late modern (not postmodern) subjectivity.

Finally, I wish to consider the postmodern mourning-work undertaken in the novels of Graham Swift – particularly *Last Orders*[14] – in order to read the novel in the light of mourning understood as the attempt, *after the return to the mother as a sort of mother/father*, to imagine a form of symbolic law (and even political practice) in which disciplinary power is mediated, responsive and continually called to account, rather than over-managing and over-intrusive; and in which juridical power is able to accommodate complexity and specificity within a wider, universal, commitment to certain rights and obligations. This involves a different way of understanding what reason, and hence a rational and just law, is. I will argue that in Winnicott's notion of perpetually responsive and adaptive 'holding'; in Swift's exploration of the transforming powers of pilgrimage as mourning; and in Gillian Rose's idea of the 'broken middle' in *Mourning Becomes the Law*;[15] we can find attempts to imagine a consciously renegotiated relationship between power (however it appears) and its subjects, in which the former is not conceived in terms of 'mastery' and the 'father' but in terms of the 'new tradition' of the father/mother which Schreber's *Memoirs* tried to inaugurate. In Gillian Rose's terms, this would be the *'the comedy of absolute spirit as inaugurated mourning'*[16], which flows – away from the melancholia of Walter Benjamin's *Trauerspiel* – towards the wry comedy of the reason and muddle in which we ordinarily, and politically, really live. All these, all too human, senses of middles and muddles strive to imagine, and make possible again, the communal *acceptance* of 'orders, rites, and procedures' which are meaningful.

CLOSER MY GOD TO THEE / O SURPLUS, OBSCENE FATHER!

Perhaps one of the most important effects of Enlightenment modernity lies in the significance it accords to ordinary lives. As is evident from Kant's essay 'What is Enlightenment?', from henceforth knowledge and power (and, thus, autonomy and political agency) is not to reside only with the aristocracy, but is to become the responsibility of ordinary people.[17] On its part, the enlightened state will undertake to reform itself in terms of its legal (and gradually political) conception of its subjects – all of whom are to be regarded, in principle, as equal or the same before the law, at least in their rights to the public exercise of critique. Recognition of this principled right and equality led, more or less inexorably by one route or another over time, to the political equality of subjects before the law. In other words, the Kantian Enlightenment principle which stated what should be the ideal legal relationship between the liberal state and its subjects ultimately produced the impetus for the state to want to know as much as possible about its populations and subjects, and to ensure the production of subjects capable of acceding to their responsibilities as bearers of such political rights.

The medico-pedagogical system prescribed by Daniel Paul Schreber's father, Dr Daniel Gottlob Moritz Schreber, physician and widely influential educationalist, described precisely such a regime. In 1858 he published a book, *Kallipädie*, which outlined a system of education for children aimed at fostering in them the central values of Enlightenment ideology and culture, and above all a sense of individual moral agency and autonomy. The programme covered nutrition, movement and exercise, sleeping habits, posture, hygienic practices, and forms of play. As Santner comments, 'Moritz Schreber's program offers a practical guide for fostering the proper metabolization – conversion into second 'nature' – of the principles and values of enlightened Christian culture. It is, in short, a systematic training program for the Enlightenment, a kind of instruction manual for parents to supplement Kant's philosophical formulation of Enlightenment values.'[18]

In his analysis Santner draws upon Freud's reading of Schreber's *Memoirs of My Nervous Illness*, in terms of a flooding of homosexual feelings – a 'homosexual panic' – in a late nineteenth-century culture which relied upon homosocial connections as its 'social glue'; he also draws on subsequent research by William Niederland on Schreber's father,[19] and on work by Friedrich Kittler on his psychiatrist at Leipzig, Paul Flechsig.[20] He argues that Schreber's paranoid schema of the split God mirrors precisely the dilemma of authority in Enlightenment. Schreber's versions of God are of one who is distant, who knows little or nothing of human beings, and is, thus, 'in accord with the law', and another God who is too close, whose 'rays' get tangled up in Schreber's 'rays', and who is 'obscenely involved in the affairs of sentient human beings: their sexual pleasures, their most private thoughts and dreams, even their bowel movements'.[21] This latter version of God is, thus, 'not in accord with the law or the Order of the World'.

This 'split God' illustrates Freud's description of paranoia as a tendency to produce splitting. Here, in particular, it is the father who is split. Santner says that it is possible to argue that, 'the entire "plot" of the *Memoirs* revolves around Schreber's attempt to integrate these two fathers, to find a way to reconcile the "outlaw" or extralegal paternal presence – the "surplus" father – with the father identified with the Order of the World and the law of proper distances'.[22] In order to discern the 'historical truth' of this surplus and obscene father, and the 'specific historical conditions under which such a figure comes to exercise his power',[23] Santner turns to the arguments of *Discipline and Punish*, and *History of Sexuality: Part 1*. In these works Foucault concludes that when the legal jurisdiction over subjects begins to interest itself in the details of the individual's life – so that, for instance, imprisonment is no longer simply punishment, but is a means of right training and the production of panoptic, self-regulating, subjects – we are 'at the threshold of modernity'.[24] With this, the juridical power necessary to the *symbolic* functions of 'deployment of alliance', to marriage systems, to kinship ties, and the transmission of names, titles, and possessions, is no longer simply distant, but operates through micro-techniques focusing upon closely attentive sexualisation of the body.[25] Enlightenment disciplinary power undermines Enlightenment juridical power. Thus, Santner says, Foucault's account of modernity as the intimate and sexualised power/knowledge of the body and its pleasures finds an eerie prefiguration in the secret history of modernity which both Schreber's *Memoirs*, and his (finally successful) legal representations for discharge from the asylum at Sonnestein in July 1901, describe.[26] Thus Schreber's struggle with 'the obscene, surplus father' is a struggle with the obscene surplusness – the much-too-closeness – of a paternal law which, in Flechsig (according to Kittler) is manifested in a mechanistic late nineteenth-century view of the relationship between the brain and the mind, and in Moritz Schreber (according to Niederland) is manifested in the 'symbiotic father' who usurps the maternal role in a domineering – and sadistic as well as benevolent – fashion. In destroying a necessary distance between power and its objects – which might be described as attentiveness to the needs of a person's soul – both these 'fathers' committed what Schreber described as 'soul murder'.

Drawing upon Foucault's distinction between Enlightenment's laudable 'ethical, political and juridical' project (in which the law operates at a critical distance from any particular body, and treats all subjects disinterestedly), and the development of intimate micro-techniques of power (in which the law intervenes intimately in the correction and right training of specific bodies), which paradoxically springs from the same Enlightenment impulse to reform, Santner argues that these close paternalistic interventions produce an excess or surplus excitation – a 'productivity' – which exceeds, and indeed threatens, the coolly rational subject which Enlightenment imagines.

As Santner argues, Foucault's work on the conflicting impulses of Enlightenment suggests that 'the disciplinary side of Enlightenment culture represents a chronic endangerment to its ethical, political, and juridical project'.[27] Perversely, the kind of overly close attention to the details of a child's intimate life displayed in Moritz Schreber's 'pedagogy for the production of disciplined enlightenment citizens' does not produce these citizens at all. On the contrary, and in its lack of attention to spontaneity and freedom, what it 'produces' (a kind of aberrant 'productivity') are 'monstrosities'.

In sum, the argument Santner makes is that Schreber's psychosis tells the story, albeit in distorted form, of modernity as the advent of *fathers who knew too much* about living human beings'.[28] To put it another way: there is something psychotic, or psychosis inducing, about the father – perhaps even about normative masculinity, since the main focus of Humanist and Enlightenment pedagogy remained the boy child – as these roles come to be imagined and enacted, in changing ways, from the end of the eighteenth century onwards. This is a large claim, and perhaps one should temper it a little. Santner's point, as I take it, is not that modernity induces something psychotic on the surface, clearly visible as it was in Schreber's exemplary case, but that – in the 'secret history of modernity' – something psychotic is present but *hidden*. The normative subject of Enlightenment proceeds 'as if' normal, but 'something is wrong'.

HIDDEN MONSTERS

Hélène Deutsch's 1942 paper 'Some Forms of Emotional Disturbance and their Relationship to Schizophrenia' derives from psychoanalytic considerations of the condition known as depersonalisation. This latter condition first gained concerted psychoanalytic attention in the early mid 1930s, and Deutsch's 1942 paper itself draws upon papers she had given earlier, in 1934 and 1938. But whilst depersonalisation refers to conditions in which the individual is aware of a sense of a lack of reality – either within him or herself, or in the world –

Deutsch's paper deals with cases in which the individuals are not aware of their lack of normal affective bonds and responses. With these individuals, their emotional disturbance is perceived only by those around them, or is first detected in analytic treatment'.[29] Deutsch calls this type of personality the 'as if' personality:

> My only reason for using so unoriginal a label for the type of person I wish to present is that every attempt to understand the way of feeling and manner of life of this type forces on the observer the inescapable impression that the individual's whole relationship to life has something about it which is lacking in genuineness and yet outwardly runs along 'as if' it were complete. Even the layman sooner or later enquires, after meeting such an 'as if' patient: what *is* wrong with him, or her?[30]

Apart from the strange (uncanny) sense that 'something is wrong', the 'as if' person seems normal, or even gifted, intellectually and emotionally. But, says Deutsch, despite all this, 'something intangible and indefinable obtrudes between the person and his fellows and invariably gives rise to the question, "What is wrong"?'[31] What psychoanalysis reveals is a person whose relationships, whilst bearing 'all the earmarks of friendship, love, sympathy and understanding' are 'devoid of any trace of warmth'.[32] As with the 'pod people' of 1950s 'social science fiction' and the replicants of 1970s, 1980s and 1990s popular film, the 'as if' person *imitates* normal affective behaviour; but, in the absence of true affect and, thus, of any moral sense derived from normal affective identifications, they exhibit their pathology in the abnormal ease with which they can switch from imitation of, or compliance with, one way of life, school of thought, or person, to another. This renders them 'capable of the greatest fidelity and the basest perfidy. Any object will do as a bridge for identification'.[33] The identifications of 'as if' lead to what Deutsch calls an 'automaton-like identification', and to the appearance of a compliant passivity which lends 'an air of negative goodness, of mild amiability'[34] reminiscent of the human-like doll Olympia in Hoffman's *The Sandman* which features in Freud's essay on the uncanny.

Donald Winnicott's version of the 'as if' personality appears in his idea of the 'false self'. This is produced by a failure of 'good enough' mothering. With reference to Jacques Lacan's 'The Mirror Stage', Winnicott argues that the role of the mother is to mirror the child back to itself. Most 'actually existing mothers' will know precisely what this means; it means the detailed responsiveness, the seductive loving, talking, and caring, which is the normal stuff of what Winnicott calls 'the ordinary devoted mother'. It is the responsiveness and 'mirroring' of the other in order to call it into being as a whole loved and live person which one observes in people who are truly in love – which, of course, the 'ordinary devoted mother' is. The mother is not 'good enough' when she is depressed, marginalised, or usurped by orders from elsewhere. The depressed (affectively deadened) mother cannot respond fully to her child and for Winnicott, as for Deutsch, this leads to the compliant infant whose only way of getting into a relation to the mother and the world is, instead of an erotic oedipal struggle, passive compliance with the mother's depressed mode of being:

> A second characteristic of such patients is their suggestibility ... Like the capacity for identification, this suggestibility ... is unlike that of the hysteric for whom object cathexis is a necessary condition; in the 'as if' individual the suggestibility must be ascribed to passivity and automaton-like identification.[35]

As with Deutsch, who stresses the essential uncreativity of the 'as if' personality, so too for Winnicott the 'false self' lacks an essentially *creative* potential; it is conventional and imitative. Adam Phillips gives an account of 'false Self' organisation in his book on Winnicott. As he describes, one of Winnicott's demands of the mother is that she is robust – if she is in any way rejecting, the infant has to comply with her response. Winnicott calls the strategies of compliance adopted by the infant the False Self organisation. Because of this primary and enforced attentiveness to the needs of the mother, the False Self always lacks something, and that something is 'the *essential element of creative originality* ... The good enough mother meets the omnipotence of the infant and to some extent makes sense of it ... The mother who is not good enough is not able to implement the infant's omnipotence, and she repeatedly fails to meet the infant's gesture, instead she substitutes her own gesture which is to be given sense by the compliance of the infant'[36] If the mother is unable to respond to the infant through identification, it must compulsively comply in order to survive. The False Self organisation, at its most extreme, 'results in a feeling unreal or a sense of futility'.[37]

Winnicott's 'False Self' is the result of the mother's failure (the sources of which have to be sought elsewhere) to meet and, over time, to manage, the infant's omnipotence. At its worst, this failure of the oedipal structure leads to the omnipotent denial of reality which is psychosis; at 'best' it leads to the *hidden* inhumanity of the apparently normal 'as if'.

In *Eros and Civilization*, Marcuse argued that resistance to the oppressive rationality of modernity required a deeper connectedness to reality – a sort of good narcissism. But the cost of untranslated narcissistic omnipotence is psychosis; the failure of the oedipus and, hence, of the institution of the principle of reality and social relations, is madness:

> An earlier generation of Left Freudians had to confront the theory of aggression to counter Freud's political pessimism. Today, precisely because we are so aware of narcissistic-preoedipal development, progressive psychoanalysts have to take up the problem of omnipotence. Any scheme for radical social transformation that does not include a mechanism for decentering infantile omnipotence stands condemned of utopianism in the pejorative sense.[38]

As a scheme for radical social transformation, the Enlightenment generally encouraged and invested in the 'mechanism' of the bourgeois family for precisely such a purpose. But what Santner's book argues is that that mechanism – which requires an engaged and affectively strong mother (or someone performing that robustly persistent function of gentle and closely attentive care), and a distant-until-later father (or anyone who is *eventually* and *in good time* consistently perceived as an obstacle to any vestiges of primary narcissism) – too often *failed*.

Aside from the question of historical detail in relation to familial practices (to which I will come shortly), the *implication* of Santner's argument is that fathers who intrude too quickly impede or evacuate what both Winnicott and Kristeva describe as 'the transitional function of the Maternal'.[39] In the 'normal' pattern of development, the infant's sense of its own omnipotence is initially mediated through its joyous or ecstatic merging with the mother who manages it. Only then upon this self-coming-to-be – a self promised in the maternal mirror – is the final *coup de grâce* of castration and repression delivered: 'I' can become my image and, in my mourning for the mother, my image will become me. But if this 'stage' of mediation is excluded, and if the father comes too close too soon, the terrifying immediacy of his castrative demand for 'renunciation' is made upon a child who has never been promised anything resembling a self by way of joyous mediations.[40] Without promise, but called into being anyway, omnipotence unmediated can only respond by splitting: on the one hand, an omnipotent denial of reality (the demand to *be* is meaningless); and, on the other hand (since one apparently *has to be* in this meaningless world), an affectless compliance, in which the child is called into being as a self which is hollowed out by a huge infantile omnipotence, but empty. This 'false self' can only receive the appearance of affective content by being shaped 'from without' as it were, whether by the delusional system or by imitative identification. This self is spoken from elsewhere with a vengeance.

THE FATHER AND THE STATE: FASCISM

As Joel Whitebook points out, for Adorno and Horkeimer the autonomous subject of Enlightenment theorised by Freud was 'a product of the "short intermezzo of liberalism"', perhaps exemplified in Thomas Arnold's pedagogical leadership at Rugby, and typified in the relationship between Thomas and his son Matthew. The latter, it will be remembered, was singularly responsible for the persuasive advocacy, in the mid-nineteenth century, of an education in culture for the rapidly swelling, philistine and often Dissenting, middle classes:

> The old Frankfurt school argued that, for a brief historical – and necessarily self-liquidating – moment, classical bourgeois society had articulated a vision of autonomy in its philosophy and high culture ...[41]

In other words, the hand-in-hand development of free markets and civil society, and of the modern family (as opposed to the pre-modern household), largely withdrawn from civil society and presided over by a strong and educated father, produced a psychical dynamic (as theorised by Freud) capable (at best) of producing sons who would reproduce all the father's 'habits of moral rectitude, cultivated taste, and critical thinking, which are the constituents of individual autonomy.'[42] As Whitebook points out, '*Homo Oeconomicus* and *Homo Criticus* were not entirely unrelated'.[43] Drawing with praise upon the system of state education in post-Revolutionary France, Matthew Arnold's proposals for the acculturation of the middle classes could be said to be a scheme for producing good fathers – the child being father to the man – as much as good sons.

Adorno and Horkheimer believed that, in the transition from liberal *laissez-faire* to administered monopoly capitalism, this strong and cultivated father was diminished by the imperative of fitting into a large, bureaucratic organisation to become merely a 'cog in the machine'.[44] This meant that his function of mediation between psyche and society (the source of the oedipal injunction to redirect, channel and defer desire [sublimate] in the service of the social good, and in a mode characterised by identification with the benevolent paternal qualities noted above) was dangerously undermined. The consequences of this, some have argued, are seen in the gradual increase in narcissistic personality disorders in which individuals lack internalised ego structures and suffer from a weak sense of distinction between self and other.

The 'good' father produced by that short intermezzo of liberalism might – where he managed to persist through the nineteenth century – be in decline in the twentieth, but, on Santner's argument, this 'good father' who judiciously produced Enlightenment subjects was already always inclined to be 'bad' because of the disciplinary element integral to the Enlightenment impulse itself. This 'good/bad' father himself had effected an earlier decline: before the decline of the good-father-turning-bad came the decline, or evacuation of influence, of the mother.

Adorno's Arnoldian father is palpably the good father, the father who observes a proper distance (invoking a respect that must be mutual) between himself and his son. But in order to accommodate Santner's reading of the 'secret' of Schreberian modernity and to correct the paternalist bias of the Freudian account (which remains caught in the 'mastering' mode of nineteenth-century technique, and maintains female subjugation in a different way), it is necessary to pursue an alternative version of the sources of what appears to be a disturbing change in the psychical structure of late modern selves. In doing so, it is important to ask about the trajectory of the 'bad father' who personifies the disciplinary aspect of Enlightenment culture. The Arnoldian 'good father' – of literary cultural traditions (in place of religion) and proper critical distances (in acknowledgement of enlightened thought) – was always under threat of marginalisation from the 'bad father', whose first literary manifestation (including maternal usurpation) is certainly Victor Frankenstein.

Whitebook believes that some credence is given to Adorno's 'exaggerations' concerning the importance of the ideal 'good bourgeois father' by the increasing emergence from the 1950s of 'preoedipal, narcissistic, and borderline disorders'[45]. But Santner's point is that the pathological state of affairs identified in the increasing emergence of borderline personalities is immanent in modernity itself – even if the narcissism this produced was not simply the neurotic's partially failed repression, but was always potentially the absolute denial of affect which characterises psychosis and its borderline variants:

Whitebook argues that many of the most important controversies within psychoanalysis since the 1950s have centred on its 'widening scope'. There has been a trend away from the 'ideal-typical "classical patient" ... who suffered from oedipal-level neurotic pathology – for example, obsessions, hysteria, phobias, and inhibitions – and for whom classical psychoanalytic technique had supposedly been designed'. Instead, 'a new type of patient has been appearing in the consulting room with increasing regularity. This patient typically suffers from preoedipal, narcissistic, and borderline character disorders – often centring on problems in separation-individuation and the coherence of the self – and must be treated with postclassical techniques.' Whitebook notes that some analysts – those informed by an awareness of disciplines such as sociology – have traced 'these new disorders' to wider transformations that have taken place in the postwar period, in the family, sex roles, socialisation, and child rearing. He also notes that these shifts have been accompanied by increasing interest in the preoedipal stages of development, and the relationship to the early mother.[46]

Santner's point is that, as with the postmodern, this state of things is immanent in modernity itself – even if it takes some time for the 'hidden' psychosis to 'appear' in the manner, and on the scale, noted by Whitebook above. And, to pick up on Adorno's 'exaggeration', although the father's mode of mediation might have changed in the early twentieth century, it did not vanish. We do not think that twentieth-century Western societies are not patriarchal; we merely notice that patriarchal disciplinary power is becoming more diffuse, operating through the company, the corporation and the apparatuses of the state, rather than simply through the ur-model which generates their relations – the nineteenth-century bourgeois family. The 'short intermezzo' was an *ideal* moment. In fact the father of modernity was and, at least until the 1950s *remained*, intrusive – albeit in different modalities.

We are on extremely difficult ground here, not least since, from the mid-1990s, anxieties about the family, parental functions, and the relationship between these and the moral health of children and society more broadly, have reached a crescendo in public debate which seems unlikely to decline in the near future. The focus of these anxieties falls inevitably upon marginal groups (single parents, the poor), but the argument presented so far suggests that the true source of the problem lies at the heart of the structure of the bourgeois family itself – in whatever modality this is historically played out.

The idea that the influence of the father should be all-pervasive in domestic as well as public life is inextricably linked to the rise of the bourgeoisie. In spite of the 'short intermezzo' in which the good, strong father is deemed central to achieving the necessary repressions required by the work ethic in complex modern societies, Santner's argument is that this father, in effect, is *psychically* dangerous inasmuch as he evacuates the mother from the field of early infant care – or at least radically weakens or undermines her influence. Further, it is surely not possible to ignore the relationship between this earlier dangerous father (whom Adorno and Horkheimer suppose to be made impotent by early twentieth-century capitalism) and the figure of the strong and dangerous father re-emerging – contemptuous of capitalist democracy but certainly not of capitalism *per se* – in the fascism in the 1920s; this is a point which Marina Warner draws out and elaborates in her 1988 novel *The Lost Father*, in which Mussolini symbolically enacts a marriage with the women of Italy.

Neither should one ignore the ways in which capitalist modernisation was reflected in technical modernisation, especially in terms of the modern weaponry of the First World War, in ways which quite radically increased a sense of male impotence manifested – famously, in the war neuroses which are the theme of Pat Barker's *Regeneration* and the source of Freud's theorisation of the death drive. It was also against this more immediate background of nineteenth-century *fin de siècle* and early twentieth-century 'flight from masculinity' that fascism attempted to reassert symbolically strong 'fathers'. Indeed, it may be the case that the weakness of the father which the Frankfurt school identified with the growth of corporate capitalism needs to be thought about in close conjunction with the symbolic movement of the father across the series family – corporation – state, which is found most clearly in fascism. In other words, corporate capitalism may make the father weak in one sense, but, when it combines directly with the state, it reproduces him on a monumental, monstrous (and thus perhaps really more truthful) scale in the politics of fascism.

It is also arguable that recognition of this series of symbolic move-ments was responsible for the (re)*turn to the mother*, in the 1940s, 1950s and beyond, as a form of *resistance* to an inner totalitarian logic of capitalist modernity perceived as inimical to the better impulses of Enlightenment and democracy. In other words, if the father of Enlightenment turned out to be a 'split' father, in which the over-proximate 'bad' father distorted and undermined the paternal function *as law* itself, then recognition of his deformations, especially as these were manifested in the political formation of fascism, *and his replacement by the mother*, far from being something to be nostalgi-cally lamented (as the Frankfurt school was inclined to do[47]), might well be thought of as an attempt to restore sanity.

NEGATIVE THEOLOGIES

I think it is quite possible to see post-war psychoanalytic emphases on the importance of the good-enough mother as locally true *and* culturally symptomatic at the same time. This double conception (psychoanalytic and cultural) was certainly held by Winnicott, and can be seen clearly in his 'The Location of Cultural Experience', where the mother is both what she is within the localised dynamic of the family and *also* a powerful figure for the possibility of cultural experience generally.

Arguments such as these necessarily hang rather uncomfortably between the psycho-symbolic and the psycho-social: the mother is both what she is in the world, and a powerful symbol – in Western cultures at least – of transitional functions. As a successful therapist of 'holding', Winnicott, I imagine, would have been one of the last people to say that men could not be nurturing; but the force of what has been argued so far is that modernity makes something particu-larly distressing of normative masculinity. It is this, rather than simply the rebarbative Second Wave feminist argument about women's need to escape from biology, that presents the real difficulty for human relations and understandings, which, generally, remain divided along powerful (gendered) models of activity and passivity, mastery and subservience. Pat Barker is right when, in her novel *Regeneration*, she has the First World War psychoanalyst Dr Rivers say that if men cannot find an authentic sense of nurturing in them-selves – rather than simply the inauthentic, and perhaps envious, copying of the *couvade* – then there is 'really very little hope'.

However, while not wishing to minimise these notable difficulties (which I leave – 'Let other pens dwell on guilt and misery'), my concern here is to explore what 'mothering' means – in the cultural life of modernity – to the pursuit of human autonomy and political freedom, particularly the latter, given the increasing perception that it was under threat from the 1940s and 1950s onwards.

The increasing psychoanalytic interest in symbolisations of the mother (as evinced in the work of Melanie Klein for instance), and then, from the 1940s, the developing interest in borderline states in which neurotic symptoms appear as a defence against psychotic breakdown, seems culturally significant. In the post World War Two years, Winnicott's notion of the False Self, with its clear echoes of Deutch's 'as if' personality, tied this unrealised, uncreative self directly into a failure to provide good-enough mothering.

Of course, it was psychoanalysis itself, with its emphasis upon the importance of affective life and the damage caused by too great a repressiveness, which was largely responsible for the challenge, made during the 1930s, to earlier, harshly utilitarian and scientistic models of the proper relationship between parent and child. When one contemplates the very normal fondness of mothers for their infants, it is hard not to see the bossy scientific approach outlined below as a terrible violence upon the natural affections of mothers and small children. As Hugh Cunningham argues, 'For much of the first half of the twentieth century the tone of advice literature presents a considerable challenge to anyone claiming that this was "the century of the child". The impact of science was to encourage in parents a distancing of parent and child.' Cunningham describes the attempts which began at around the end of the nineteenth century to subjugate child rearing to exact, scientifically founded, rules: 'In 1914 the United States Children's Bureau was advising that "The rule that parents should not play with the baby may seem hard, but it is without doubt a safe one". In the United States John Watson was in no doubt that there were "much more scientific ways of bringing up children" ... his advice was uncompromising ... "Never hug and kiss them, never let them sit in your lap".[48]

However, as Cunningham argues, with the influence of psychoanalysis this repressive mode of child-rearing, encapsulated in the notion of training, began to be associated with fascism, while attempts to understand the child and work with it were associated with democracy'.[49] This is the association which Winnicott, in 1957, also makes:

> In the last half century there has been a great increase in awareness of
> the value of the home ... We know something of the reasons why this
> long and exacting task, the parent's job of seeing their children
> through, is a job worth doing; and in fact, we believe that it provides
> the only real basis for society, and the only factory for the democratic
> tendency in a country's social system.[50]

For Winnicott, pole position in the 'parent's job', it is clear, goes to
the mother. In the beginning, the good father's job is protecting the
mother so that she can love her child in an uninterrupted, and un-
interfered with, way. The mother, therefore, becomes the figure
through which democracy can be protected from fascism. But, as we
have seen, this fascism is not simply the fascism of 'abroad'; there is
something in liberal utilitarianism, in the home-grown doctrine of
Enlightenment itself, which is fascistic and 'psychotic'. In this equa-
tion, scientific and utilitarian rationality stand on the same side as
over-invasive scientistic paternity and madness; the non-calculable
devotion of the ordinary mother stands on the side of democracy.
There is thus some truth in criticisms of 1950s science fiction which
argue that it depicts 'the enemy within' in terms of a political formation (communism); but this might itself be regarded as a
quasi-psychotic denial and projection. The real enemy within capitalist countries is fascism, and this returns 'from without' as the threat
of a totalitarian other named as communism.

The problem of liberal Enlightenment, as Adorno well knew,
becomes that of imagining how the orderings (and repressions) necessary to the rational conduct of civic life and political freedom can be
achieved in a non-violent non-totalitarian way; a way which doesn't
distort a sense of human-ness, 'the feeling of being a person in the
world'. The answer offered by Winnicott is that a non-violent, non-
mastering 'togetherness of the manifold' can be achieved by making
space for the mother's way of doing things, because she is *now*
perceived as combining both an anarchic, playful capacity *and* a law-
making one, in which some semantic, symbolic stability is also
achieved.

For Julia Kristeva also, the excision of meaningful symbolisations
of the mother stems from the Reformation. Before this, and as
Kristeva notes, 'the most intense revelation of God, which occurs in
mysticism, is given only to a person who assumes himself as 'maternal'... Augustine, Bernard of Clairvaux, Meister Eckhart, to mention
but a few, played the part of the Father's virgin spouses, or even, like

Bernard, received drops of virginal milk directly on their lips.' As Kristeva goes on to argue:

> Freedom with respect to the maternal territory then becomes the pedestal upon which love of God is erected. As a consequence, mystics, those 'happy Schrebers' (Sollers) throw a bizarre light on the psychotic sore of modernity: it appears as the incapability of contemporary codes to tame the maternal, that is, primary narcissism. Uncommon and 'literary', their present day counterparts are always somewhat oriental, if not tragical – Henry Miller who says he is pregnant, Artaud who sees himself as 'his daughters' or 'his mother' ... It is the orthodox constituent of Christianity ... that sanctioned *the transitional function of the Maternal* by calling the Virgin a 'bond', a 'middle' or an interval, thus opening the door to more or less heretical identifications with the Holy Ghost (emphasis mine).[51]

Whatever the dubious origins of the idea of the *Virgin* Mother in a mistranslation, for Kristeva, 'Western Christianity has organized that "translation error", projected its own fantasies into it and produced one of the most powerful imaginary constructs known in the history of civilizations'.[52] That Mary, 'maternality' and the locus of materiality impregnated (which is to say the soul within the compass of reason), is thought of as a 'middle' and in the form of a 'bond', or the productive identificatory space linking God and world, is surely significant. This mystical, uncanny space of mediated identification appears as a sort of medieval version of Winnicottian 'transitional space' which, equally uncanny, is a 'neither inside nor outside'[53] space, but one in which, through the first use of a symbol – the first play – the infant's experience of being merged with the mother finds a way of projecting itself into the world as a symbol (transitional object) *of* the mother. From this primary transitional function all successful and creative symbolic life can flow:

> The [transitional] object is a symbol of the union of the baby and the mother (or part of the mother). This symbol can be located. It is at the place in space and time where and when the mother is in transition from being (in the baby's mind) merged in with the infant and alternatively being experienced as an object to be perceived rather than conceived of. The use of an object symbolizes the union of two now separate things, baby and mother, *at the point in time and space of the initiation of their state of separateness*.[54]

In secular modernity, it is, thus, significant that Winnicott seeks to re-establish whatever it is that mothers symbolise and do, as being at the centre of the possibility of wholesome cultural experience and 'making', generally. In his essay 'The Location of Cultural Experience', the mother, in her 'holding' of the transitional space in which traditional meanings are subject to creative change and making in the infant's use of transitional objects, is more of a *father/mother*. She is both eventual upholder of the law (she *will* bring the child to more or less fixed meanings, potty-training and the 'law' of reason), and a *subversive* – in her committed collusions with and adaptations to the child, and in her readiness to join in the anarchy of play, and to respond to the irrational or teasing demands imposed by the child whom she loves.

In 'The Location of Cultural Experience' we see that what the mother and infant do is a work of mourning; but, importantly, it is also intensely creative; it is a work of art in which the infant *makes* symbols (transitional objects), and in which words and meanings can, as in Hélène Cixous's 'realm of the gift', 'fly' or be 'stolen'.[55] Jay Bernstein argues that, in modernity, art is always also mourning-work,[56] but in Winnicott's description of transitional spaces and phenomena, we see this as communicative action in the real world.

As Whitebook points out, for Adorno the advanced work of art, refusing easy aesthetic pleasures, requires us to feel and think at the same time. It asks us to surrender to a sensual difficulty (of form, line, tonality or association) in order to make us pay attention to the relation between intellect (symbolic abstraction) and body (sensation/'aesthetic' pleasure or unpleasure), and the possibility of uniting these. In other words, the work of art which unmans you (or, as a defence, bores, or irritates, you), by turning your legs to water and your mind to mulch, is a work of art potentially capable of bringing two (in modernity) incompatible modes of thought together in a non-violent, non-mastering, way. The heart which sinks, whilst the mind obliges it forward in its sinking, is, for Adorno, a model of 'the non-violent togetherness of the manifold'[57] through, or in, which modernity might be redeemed from its destructive divisions and dualisms.

This kind of psychical movement – of conscious surrender to an idea as a strategy of advance (another way of describing which might simply be 'intellectual empathy') – might seem feminine or obscure, but Winnicott seems to imply that we find something like a model of the production of good culture (a creative and emancipated space) in the transitional space in which mothers and infants mourn and make. The Winnicottian mother is a modernist whose mediations play to the best impulses of Enlightenment. Adorno thought that any rationality, including discursive rationality, must be oppressive and distorting so that the aim of Enlightenment – to increase human happiness and freedom – must always be undermined by the mode of mastery and self-mastery that it necessarily employs. But, for Winnicott at least, the production of autonomy and reason in the child must always involve engaged processes in which symbols – words and meanings – are much more fluid, and are playfully (though very seriously) negotiated. As in Albrecht Wellmer's description of communicative reason, there is a 'moving back and forth between concept and object' and 'between one concept of an object and another'.[58] Interestingly, it's worth noting that both of these mobile and playful versions of reason and communication accord very well with the model of mind (or I should say, mind/body) found in the theories of contemporary neurobiology which I discuss in chapter 5.

Winnicott calls what the mother does 'holding'. As Adam Phillips points out, 'Where Freud sees the possibility for mastery, Winnicott sees the possibility for surprise. Where Freud is preoccupied with defensive forms of control, Winnicott emphasizes something less virile, which he calls "holding". "Holding" describes the early maternal care that makes possible the infant's psychosomatic integration; and holding implies reciprocal accommodations, exactly what one observes in the subtle process of someone's carrying or picking up a child'.[59] In other words, one of the things that the mother, or mothering, might mean, or have come to mean, in late modernity is the practical possibility (or the model of a practical possibility), in the middle of things in the real world, of a form of rationality (for mothers certainly have their reasons) which is, nevertheless, non-calculable and essentially non-violent. That is to say that ordinary mothers, for mundane and tired, as well as loving reasons, certainly calculate effects; but their procedures are imaginative and in the moment of the day to day and the face to face; no utilitarian rule or childcare handbook could compass them. They are subversive calculations which resist any totalising calculation.

In the next sections of this chapter I aim to develop further an understanding of the nature of this subversion – of what appears to be a form of reason not amenable to the codifying demands of utilitarian rationality, a sort of broken middle between reason and affect, or between what Gillian Rose calls 'the city and the soul', in which rites, orders and procedures might once again be invested with meaning. I want to do this through turning to Graham Swift's 1996 novel, *Last Orders*, which I will read together with a part of Rose's *Mourning Becomes the Law*. In doing this, I will be arguing that what the transitional space does, and what the mother does, and what working in the 'broken middle' does, is the same as what Winnicott calls 'holding'; and I will argue that that this being in the middle of real things, and holding them, is actually what, as real human beings, we're *really* made of; our intelligence, our art and our science, do not spring from calculations abstracted from bodies, affects and other real things in the world, but are the condition of being in the middle of these things. This is what neurobiologist Antonio Damasio describes in terms of a mind-body continuum; it is what mathematician Keith Devlin describes as the world-situatedness of mind;[61] and it is what philosopher Gillian Rose calls 'the broken middle'. For Swift, it is mourning accomplished in the labour and muddle, gamble and risk of being in the middle of real things.

What I am arguing is that Humanism (which begins in the fifteenth century but which finds its feet in Enlightenment Modernity in the eighteenth century) has an *idea* of the human which, in its eagerness to modernise, and its thirst for knowledge and earthly power, it almost immediately, inadvertently, stamps out. The humanism of Enlightenment modernity becomes, thus, quite quickly a sort of inhumanism; but it bequeaths to us an idea of what it might be like to be a fully autonomous human being. It follows, then, that if Humanism – and Enlightenment – is already contaminated with something psychotic and inhuman, to be human *after* Humanist Enlightenment would be to become more truly human according to the ideal imagined (but almost immediately distorted by the advent of 'fathers who wanted to know too much') in the fifteenth century. To talk about the end of Humanism, or the 'end of man', might possibly be to inaugurate the human as more fully human: a new humanism, and a new 'second' modernity, as Wellmer puts it.

I have argued elsewhere that the postmodern might usefully be understood as the meeting between modern melancholia and a mourning – rather than an increasing psychosis that late modernity could become – so that *mourning* becomes the postmodern.[62] In an argument which seems right to me, Wellmer suggests that, with postmodernism, the critique of modernity recognises that gestures of 'radical surpassing – romantic utopianism'[63] are no longer possible, and have even constituted the most totalitarian of modernity's teleological narratives. Postmodernism recognises this complicity of a certain kind of dialectical thought, and seeks, at its best, to replace it with another, which I am likening to the work of mourning. This is dogged persistent work,[64] like the dredging of the Fens in Swift's *Waterland*, but it is also a creative work of continual adaptation typified by Winnicott's notion of transitional space, or Gillian Rose's 'broken middle' between the city, the soul and the sacred.[65]

Writing of Adorno's understanding of the 'aporetic relationship between art and philosophy', or experience and criticism, Wellmer notes that, in this, 'a theological perspective is sublated: art and philosophy combine to form the two halves of a negative theology'.[66] What he means to point out is that for Adorno aesthetic intelligence is immediate – utterly 'meaningful', but untranslatable in its essence – whereas critical intelligence (philosophy) is comprehensible but emptied: 'Just as a moment of blindness adheres to the immediacy of aesthetic perception, so does a moment of emptiness adhere to the "mediacy" of philosophical thought. Only in combination are they capable of circumscribing a truth which neither alone is able to articulate. "Truth lies unveiled for discursive knowledge, but for all that, it does not possess it; the knowledge that is art has it (truth), but as something incommensurable to it".[67]

I hope I have shown that, as with the figure of the Virgin in the Middle Ages, for Winnicott the secular figure of the ordinary devoted mother holds the transitional space between knowledge (the law) and affect (love). In other words, the Winnicottian implication of *a mother who is also a father* opens up a (transitional) space in which affect is not unreasonable – the heart has its reasons – but in which calculating rationality is itself always shot through with something finally incalculable. This is, of course, and in fact, the place of 'reason and muddle' – the living space of a negative theology trying to recognise itself *as logos* – with which, as Gillian Rose says, we are actually all too familiar.[68] In his recent book on the limits of the use of mathematical, propositional logic when faced with the endless contingent muddles of a context of 'being in the middle of real things', and thus of the impossibility of reproducing human 'mind' in Artificial Intelligences, Keith Devlin makes a similar point.[69] I now wish to turn to a negative theology of the postmodern, which I believe can be discovered in the territory between the mourning-works of Gillian Rose and Graham Swift. In, or between, these works, the transitional function of the Winnicottian father/mother reappears in the movement between the city and the soul.

REASON AND AFFECT, OR, THE CITY AND THE SOUL

The law – in its always intertwined symbolic and actual dimensions – which Gillian Rose called Old Athens, must, if it is to be just and if politics is to be possible, hold the power of investiture. How can this come about? How can we, as Rose puts it, chase the spirits of our history 'back into their bodies, back into the history of their development, in order to comprehend their law and their anarchy and to complete the work of mourning?';[70] and what is the significance of finding the figure of the woman, especially as mother, as the source of a 'broken middle' between affective anarchy and rational law as Winnicott does? It seems to me that what is at work in Winnicott's turn to the mother as a site of resistance to fascism is essentially a recognition that the orthodox oedipal structure has outlived its historical moment – that brief intermezzo of liberalism – and has too often failed. But rather than abandoning the structure, Winnicott reconceives it in different terms. Perhaps a postmodern subjectivity – far from being the fractured melancholic of modernity, or the borderline psychotic of late modernity – would be a subjectivity founded symbolically and (in some cases) actually on 'mothers' and 'fathers' who had, *in some symbolic or mythic sense*, been returned to their pre-Reformation places so that the possibility of symbolising transitional spaces and phenomena as profoundly important – that is to say, the creative spaces of our souls – is restored. The way that Winnicott does this is to make the mother a *mother/father*, in which mourning and the necessary renewals of cultural life can exist in the movement *between* anarchy and law. Similarly, Gillian Rose's notion of the 'broken middle' seems to aim at the same movement and the same space.

In her discussion of the Antigone story (in which, just outside the city boundary of Athens, Antigone goes to bury brother's body, in defiance of Creon's decree, and the wife of Phocion goes to gather the ashes of her disgraced husband), Rose asks the meaning of these acts:

> Do they represent the transgression of the law of the city – women as the irony of the political community, as its ruination? Do they bring to representation an immediate ethical experience, 'women's experience', silenced and suppressed by the law of the city, and hence expelled outside its walls? No. In these delegitimate acts of tending the dead, these acts of justice, against the current will of the city, women reinvent the political life of the community.

By insisting on the right and rites of mourning, Antigone and the wife of Phocion carry out that intense work of the soul, that gradual rearrangement of its boundaries, which must occur when a loved one is lost – so as to let go, to allow the other fully to depart, and hence fully to be regained beyond sorrow. To acknowledge and to re-experience the justice and the injustice of the partner's life and death is to accept the law, it is not to transgress it – mourning becomes the law.[71]

In other words, to mourn is to reinvest the world and the self with symbolic significance (rites and orders); but it also to remember that this world will always be a radically changed one in which boundaries are, indeed, rearranged; in which rites, orders, and procedures, inasmuch as they comply with the just law, must at the same time change it. Thus, as Winnicott notes, the mourning of mother and infant is creative, but this creativity which *makes* culture depends upon the continual interplay of tradition and innovation.[72] This is how mourning becomes us. This is what we're made of.

LAST ORDERS: TO BE WHAT WE'RE MADE OF

Graham Swift's *Last Orders* is a pilgrimage. It starts at a pub in Southwark from where, eventually, a group of friends – Vic, Vince (an undertaker), Lenny (the dead Jack's adopted son, a market fruit and veg stallholder and failed boxer), and little Ray (a lucky gambler) – make their journey, via Canterbury, to Margate to scatter the ashes of their butcher friend Jack Dodds (I take the name Dodds to be an amalgamation of Dads and gods) upon the sea. As with *The Canterbury Tales*, the narrative consists of the tales of each of these pilgrims; although here, in line with the 'protestant' conventions of the English novel, these tales largely take the form of private, inner narratives. Swift's continual preoccupation with the relationship between fathers and sons reappears in *Last Orders*; but, this time, it is not with a father who will not acknowledge a son, but with an adopted son who will not acknowledge a father. As with the traditional work of elegy, the novel's drive is towards re-establishing the order in which the symbolic father, as dead father, is acknowledged by the 'son' who comes after. As Peter Sacks says, in order to succeed, the elegy must re-establish reverence for the father and the law.[73]

In his previous, 1992, novel *Ever After*, Swift explored erotic romantic love, and asked whether this is enough to help us survive ever after. His conclusion there was maybe, maybe not: it depends on how you understand the verbs 'to love', and 'to take'.[74] In *Last Orders*, the emphasis seems to fall upon the spirit with which a person finally takes command of, or orders, themselves in their loving. Here, the messiness and contingency of human lives – the gamble of it all – is subsumed within a last kind of order; but it is one *discovered* during the pilgrimage rather than imposed at the start and rigidly enforced. Jack's last orders – that he should be 'buried at sea' – seem to be the *first* orders of the day of the pilgrimage; but they are shifted in the comedy of experience, and truly *become* last orders, are fitting and becoming *as* last orders, in the remains of the day, when the friends cast him to sea upon the eventide.

Throughout the novel, characters follow the commands of love: not as desire, but rather as a kind of acknowledgement of obligations. From the same root as ligature, obligation means a binding-up, a tie. And what the pilgrimage allows each to discover is that the order expressed in last rites – in proper mourning in other words – is precisely the same order expressed in the ties of love. As in Hegel's *Phenomenology*, the movements of spirit which trace out all the follies and detours – the necessary processes of indirection – of the stages of the encounter with death and mourning turn out, in the end, to be the work of mutual recognition and obligation which is love *(caritas)* as *work* in the social and political commitments and activities of the day to day – 'activity beyond activity' as Gillian Rose puts it.

Perhaps one of the most interesting things about Swift's intricate and reverberating novel is the way in which – beneath the ordinary Bermondsey voices and lives, and embedded in both the pilgrimage form and the allegorical names of so many of the characters (Victor, Vince, Ray, Amy, and the death-bed nurse Joy) – another language surprisingly emerges. It's nothing elevated but, nonetheless, is a glimpse of the sacred and the enchanted: it is the symbolic language of the spirit and the soul. This pilgrimage passes beyond Canterbury to, of all places, Margate, where Jack and Amy Dodds took a belated honeymoon in 1939 and where, fifty years later, Jack orders his friends to bury him 'at sea'. But if the faded seaside town, and the lights of Dreamland and Marine Parade, represent a rather tired dream of England, it is nevertheless from that tacky fantasy of the pleasures of mass consumption, rather than from the cathedral mass at Canterbury, that symbolic salvation must be found. The Miracle Worker in this novel is an outsider running at 33-1: a horse. Jack, dying in hospital and in debt, asks the little Ray of hope – the lucky gambler among them – to place a bet for him. When Ray's chosen horse The Miracle Worker wins, Jack knows that his wife Amy – that is to say his 'love', or 'soul' – will be safe, and he dies leaving only the last orders for his 'burial at sea'.

And, of course it is the settling of *this* spiritual debt, rather than the calculable financial one, that will do the work of mourning. Any modern fool recognises the nature of monetary debts, but it is only in the folly of other kinds of obligation – the novel is full of 'fool's errands' and 'detours' in the service of memories and memorials – that the nature of the debt, the significance of the human comedy, and the work of mourning, will be realised symbolically. Jack's wife, Amy – so often called Ame (*Ame*, soul) – does not go on the pilgrimage. That is because she is attending, as she has done for fifty years, to her own pilgrimage, in the regular beat of the visits to the idiot daughter June, to whom Jack has refused to acknowledge any obligation. The friends undertake the pilgrimage *for* Ame – who has her own. In *Last Orders*, postmodern realism works through ordinary lives in order to realise the soul and to inaugurate mourning *for her* and on her behalf. The dead father is mourned and, in the labour of the day, reverence is not only re-established for him, but for the mother-soul also. In this, dead butcher Jack *and* living Ame 'become what we're made of':

> It's true what Vic said. The wind takes it, it's gone in a whirl, in a flash. Now you see it, now you don't. Then I take the jar in both hands again, giving a quick peek inside, and say, 'Come on, come on'. They all huddle round to take another scoop. There isn't much more than four men can scoop out twice over. They dip in again, one by one. Lucky dip. And I dip and we all throw again, a thin trail of white, like smoke, before it's gone, and some seagulls swoop in from nowhere and veer off again like they've been tricked. Then I know there's not enough for another share-out, another full round, so I just start scooping myself, they don't seem to mind. I scoop and scoop like some animal scratching out its burrow, and I know in the end I'm going to have to hold up the jar and bang it like you do when you get to the bottom of a box of cornflakes. One handful, two handfuls, there's only two handfuls. I say, 'Goodbye Jack'. The sky and the sea and the wind are all mixed up together but I reckon it wouldn't make no difference if they weren't because of the blur in my eyes. Vic and Vincey's faces look like white blobs but Lenny's looks like a beacon, and across the water you can see the lights of Margate. You can stand on the end of Margate Pier and

look across to Dreamland. Then I throw the last handful and the seagulls come back on a second chance and I hold up the jar, shaking it, like I should chuck it out to sea too, a message in a bottle, Jack Arthur Dodds, save our souls, and the ash that I carried in my hands, which was the Jack who once walked around, is carried away by the wind, is whirled away by the wind till the ash becomes wind and the wind becomes Jack what we're made of (*Last Orders*, p294-5).

It's probably worth noting that 'Jack' means both the real, living, person who once 'walked around', and also, in contemporary slang, 'nothing'. I don't think that any of this should be taken as an affirmation of what Gillian Rose called the New Jerusalem of a fantasised community at the expense of the reason of old Athens. I don't think it is Swift's purpose to argue simply for community, or 'immediate ethical experience in place of the risks of critical rationality' as Rose sharply puts it.[75] The invocation of order, of last orders, and of commands to the labour, not merely the form, of last rites, says otherwise. The point is rather, I think, that which Rose explores in her last book: that proper mourning is *only* possible in the discovery of the *just* law and in the recognition of the boundaries and civic obligations signified by the *just* city – rational Athens at its best, let us say.

I think that what Swift is ever after here, in *Last Orders*, is the recognition that the order of reason and death – the dead are all *the same* insists undertaker Vic – and the disorder of human contingency and difference displayed in the histories of the Bermondsey friends not only can but *must* be thought in the same place at the same time: the obligations imposed by the dead *are*, if we feel inclined to meet them, the obligations we discover and renegotiate in life. If we give up on the father and the law as irredeemably obscene, and if we give up on trying to discover what *just* and nonperverse forms of these might be, then all we will have left is the suicidal revenge of the melancholic, or the mad inhumanity of 'as if'.

What Swift's pilgrims come to on their fool's errand, with its constant memorial detours, is the remembrance, rediscovery and renegotiation – beyond the city walls where the ashes of the dead are left – of boundaries and of what binds us. These are what Gillian Rose calls the boundaries of the city and the soul. Discussing Sister Wendy Beckett's reading of Poussin's 'Gathering the Ashes of Phocion', Rose reminds that the Athenian law which had the virtuous Phocion cremated by an alien without the city walls, was a tyrannical law – 'tyranny temporarily usurping good rule in the city'[76] – not a just one.

In *Last Orders* the bleeding heart of the modern city is Smithfield – 'Life and death' says Jack the butcher. In his life Jack did not do justice to his obligations to June, Amy, the soul, or love; but in his *death*, by what he obliged his friends to do and to experience, for *themselves* and for *her*, he managed it – and mourning became them. Within the modern city just now – as in the Athens of Phocion – the soul and the city are ruled by butchers; but beyond the city walls, in Margate of all places, the soul becomes a trope, or trick, of the wind, which whirls around the ashes until 'the ash becomes the wind and the wind becomes Jack what we're made of'.

CULTURES OF MOURNING

From first to last, Swift's novels present an extraordinarily sustained effort to imagine Romanticism's failure to manage the successful mourning it seeks. With *Last Orders*, Swift is able, at last, to incorporate a form of the sacred expressible in terms of ordinary lives. His development of a creative engagement with the difficulties of modernity is instructive, and it is to a discussion of this engagement and to other, related cultural symptoms of the urge to mourn that I now turn.

NOTES

1   P. Barker, *Regeneration*, Penguin, Harmondsworth 1992.
2   E.L. Santner, *My Own Private Germany: Daniel Paul Schreber's Secret History of Modernity*, Princeton University Press, Princeton 1996.
3   W. Niederland, 'The Miracled-Up World of Schreber's Childhood', *The Psychoanalytic Study of the Child*, vol. XIV, Imago, London 1959; 'Further Data and Memorabilia Pertaining to the Schreber Case', *The International Journal of Psychoanalysis*, vol.44, part 2, 1963.
4   In *Parsifal*, the keeper of the holy grail and spear (Amfortas) is seduced by a bewitching woman (secretly Kundry, in one of her guises). He lets fall the spear, which is then seized by the evil Klingsor who wounds him with it and steals the spear. Amfortas's wound bleeds perpetually, and the protective task of the knights of the grail lies in ruins. This is 'the institutional domain in crisis' as Santner puts it. The spear is retrieved, and Klingsor vanquished, by Parsifal (the innocent fool) who understands his mission only at the moment when he resists Kundry's attempted seduction

of him. This seduction is, it should be noted, highly ambiguous since, in it, she is also seeking redemption. While she precipitates Amfortas's suffering (Klingsor is the true source), Kundry is also often to be found close to him, attempting to offer balm to his wound. For Wagner, the Jew is inevitably intimately bound up with modernity's story of enlightenment and redemption, but the achievement of the latter necessitates Kundry's death. The Nazi understanding of Wagnerian mythology requires, of course, no further comment from me.

5   Santner, 1996, *op. cit.* p144.

6   *Ibid.*

7   Sontag, 'Under the Sign of Saturn', *A Susan Sontag Reader*, Penguin, Harmondsworth 1983, p400.

8   Santner, 1996, *op. cit.*, pxii

9   M. Dolar, '"I Shall Be with You on Your Wedding-Night": Lacan and the Uncanny', *October*, 58, (Fall, 1991).

10 Santner, 1996, *op. cit.*, p176, n45.

11 H. Deutsch, 'Some Forms of Emotional Disturbance and their Relation to Schizophrenia', *The Psychoanalytic Quarterly*, vol.11, 1942.

12 A. LeGacy, '*The Invasion of the Body Snatchers*: A Metaphor for the Fifties', *Literature/Film Quarterly*, vol. VI, no.3, (Summer, 1978), p291.

13 D.W. Winnicott, 'The Location of Cultural Experience' [1967], in Winnicott, *Playing and Reality*, Routledge, London 1991.

14 G. Swift, *Last Orders*, Picador, London 1996.

15 G. Rose, *Mourning Becomes the Law: Philosophy and Representation*, Cambridge University Press, Cambridge 1996.

16 *Ibid.*, p76.

17 I. Kant, 'What is Enlightenment?', *Kant On History*, Lewis White Beck (ed), Bobbs-Merill, Indianapolis 1956.

18 Santner, 1996, *op. cit.*, p89 & p90.

19 Niederland, 1959, *op. cit.*

20 F. Kittler, *Discourse Networks 1800-1900*, tr. M. Meteer & C. Cullens, Stanford University Press, Stanford 1990. See in Santner, 1996, *op. cit.*, pp71ff.

21 Santner, 1996, *op. cit.*, p62.

22 *Ibid.*

23 *Ibid.*

24 M. Foucault, *The History of Sexuality: Vol. 1 – An Introduction*, tr. R. Hurley, Allen Lane, London 1979, p143.

25 Santner, 1996, *op. cit.*, p62.

26 *Ibid.*, pp80-81: Schreber argues for a separation of police and medical powers: 'In effect, Schreber is arguing that the state has no mandate

pertaining to the physical or mental *health* of its citizens. The only concern should be, as Schreber paraphrases the relevant legal principle in his writ of appeal, "whether I possess the capacity for reasonable action in practical life"'

27 *Ibid.*, pp90-91.

28 *Ibid.*, p86.

29 Deutsch, 1942, *op. cit.*, p301.

30 *Ibid.*, p302.

31 *Ibid.*, p302.

32 *Ibid.*, p303.

33 *Ibid.*, p304.

34 *Ibid.*, p305.

35 *Ibid.*

36 Cited in A. Phillips, *Winnicott*, Fontana, London 1988, pp133-4.

37 Cited in *ibid.*

38 J. Whitebook, *Perversion and Utopia: A Study in Psychoanalysis and Critical Theory*, MIT, London, 1995, p41.

39 J. Kristeva, 'Stabat Mater', *The Kristeva Reader*, Toril Moi (ed), Blackwell, Oxford 1986, p163; Winnicott, [1967] 1991, *op. cit.*

40 See Moritz Schreber's insistence on infantile 'renouncing' in M. Schatzman, *Soul Murder: Persecution in the Family*, Allen Lane, London 1973, p60: 'Consider this regimen to train a child, before he is *one*, in "self-denial". No one must give the infant a morsel of food besides the regular three meals a day. His nurse seats him on her lap while she eats or drinks whatever she wishes. However much the child should wish food or drink, she must give him none'. This paraphrases the source, which is Niederland's 'Miracled-Up World, 1959, *op. cit.*

41 Whitebook, 1995, *op. cit.*, p135.

42 *Ibid.*, p136-7.

43 *Ibid.*, p137.

44 *Ibid.*, p137.

45 *Ibid.*, p138.

46 Ibid., pp139-40.

47 *Ibid.*, p136.

48 H. Cunningham, *Children and Childhood in Western Societies Since 1500*, Longman, London 1995, p175-6.

49 *Ibid.*, p176.

50 D.W. Winnicott, *Home is Where We Start From: Essays by a Psychoanalyst*, [1957], Penguin, Harmondsworth 1986, p124.

51 Kristeva, 1986, *op. cit.*, pp162-3.

52 *Ibid.*, p163.

53 Winnicott, [1967] 1991, *op. cit.*, p96.

54 *Ibid.*, pp96-7.

55 H. Cixous, 'Sorties', in H. Cixous & C. Clement, *The Newly Born Woman*, tr. B. Wing, University of Minnesota Press, London, 1986.

56 J. Bernstein, *The Fate of Art: Aesthetic Alienation from Kant to Derrida and Adorno*, Polity, London 1992.

57 Whitebook, 1995, p154.

58 A. Wellmer, *The Persistence of Modernity: Essays on Aesthetics, Ethics, and Postmodernism*, tr. D. Midgley, MIT, Cambridge, Massachusetts 1991, p81.

59 A. Phillips, *On Kissing, Tickling and Being Bored: Psychoanalytic Essays on the Unexamined Life*, Faber & Faber, London 1993, p42.

60 A. Damasio, *Descartes' Error: Emotion, Reason and the Human Brain*, Picador, London 1994.

61 K. Devlin, *Goodbye Descartes: The End of Logic and the Search for a New Cosmology of Mind*, John Wiley, Chichester 1997.

62 W. Wheeler, 'After Grief? What Kinds of Inhuman Selves?', *New Formations*, 25, (Summer, 1995).

63 Wellmer, 1991, *op. cit.*, ppxi-xii.

64 In late 1998, BBC1's *Everyman* programme broadcast a film, 'Surviving Lockerbie' (29/11/98; producer Richard Denton) about the mourning-work associated with the aftermath of the bombing of Pan Am flight 103 over Lockerbie ten years earlier on 21 December 1988. Everyone on board the aircraft died – 270 people in the air and in the town in total. The film concerned the return to Lockerbie, ten years after the tragedy, of the American daughter of one of the victims. There she learned that her own mourning was accompanied by the tremendous, years-long labour of mourning pragmatically undertaken by the town's inhabitants. This was not only for the townsfolk who had died, but included the meticulous and painstaking forensic work undertaken by the local police over a period of three years, which made possible the identification of every single item of luggage and clothing scattered over more than a hundred square miles. Once identified, absolutely everything was cleaned, and clothes were laundered and ironed by local volunteers, so that where the families of the dead wanted to reclaim the effects (and not all did), everything belonging to the victims could be returned as cleansed of violence as humans could make it. This profoundly moving film illustrated, for me, as well as anything I have come across, the complex symbolic and practical work involved in the labour of mourning.

65 By 'broken middle', Gillian Rose means an agonistic space characterised by the exercise of 'reinvigorated, open-hearted reason' in which mourning is the word given to 'the reassessment of reason, gradually rediscovering

its own moveable boundaries'. Rose, 1996, *op. cit.*, p11. This is in many ways an essentially liberal affirmation of the importance of argumentation, opposition, or agonistics, as productive of change and renewal and, thus, as the *prerequisite* of agreement (about justice and the law in democracies), not its undoing. For Rose, the polarised politics of the 1980s and 1990s (neo-liberal or libertarian, on the one hand; communitarian or conservative on the other) exhibit forms of rigidity associated with melancholic splitting and repetition. The 'broken middle' is precisely *not* the blanketed, friction free, 'unfractured middle' suggested by Tony Blair's Third Way (which one imagines Rose would have loathed); it is, on the contrary, an agonistic space riven with risk. (See the description of the 'contorted posture of political risk' of Phocion's wife's female companion in Rose's discussion of Poussin's 'Gathering the Ashes of Phocion' which follows.)

66 Wellmer, 1991, p71.
67 *Ibid.*, p7.
68 Rose, 1996, p34.
69 Devlin, 1997, *op. cit.*
70 Rose, 1996, p71.
71 *Ibid.*, pp35-6.
72 Winnicott, [1967] 1991, *op. cit.*, p96.
73 P. Sacks, *The English Elegy: Studies in the Genre from Spenser to Yeats*, Johns Hopkins University Press, London 1985, p301.
74 See my more detailed reading of *Ever After* in Wheeler, 1995, *op. cit.* Here and subsequently, references to Graham Swift's novels appear in the text: (SSO) *The Sweet Shop Owner*, Allen Lane, London 1980; (WL) *Waterland*, Heinemann, London 1983; (EA) *Ever After*, Pan Books, London 1992; (LO) *Last Orders*, Picador, London 1996.
75 Rose, 1996, *op. cit.*, p22.
76 *Ibid.*, p25.

CHAPTER 3

From the sublime to the ridiculous
Mourning, laughter and other transitional spaces in culture

> The sublime and the ridiculous are so often nearly related, that it is difficult to class them separately. One step above the sublime makes the ridiculous; and one step above the ridiculous makes the sublime again.
>
> Tom Paine, *The Age of Reason* 1795

> What ever is funny is subversive, every joke is ultimately a custard pie ... A dirty joke is ... a sort of mental revolution.
>
> George Orwell, *The Art of Donald McGill* 1945

In the last chapter, I looked at the idea of the 'split father' in Schreber's mythology as representative of a problem about how 'power' (in the Foucauldian sense) works in modernity. I suggested that in Gillian Rose's idea of the broken middle, in Winnicott's idea of transitional space, and in Graham Swift's idea of mourning as pilgrimage, we can see the imagining of a different space, or relation, between power and its objects. Such creative agonistic 'spaces' would be characterised by the affirmation of openness, mutuality, adaptation and the valuation of critical thought, and by a commitment to communicative, *'open-hearted'*, that is *affective*, rationality.

In this chapter I will look at the novelist Graham Swift's exemplary treatment of an intensified nostalgic melancholia as a representative mode of affect in Western societies (but perhaps particularly Anglo-American ones) during the 1980s, together with his hopeful move towards forms of social solidarity, expressed in mourning and pilgrimage, in his 1996 novel *Last Orders*. The second part of the chapter will seek to widen the scope of the discussion by pursuing some other writers' ideas or examples of places or practices which evade the 'iron cage' of melancholy power.

FROM THE SUBLIME TO THE DOMESTIC: GRAHAM SWIFT – LAYING THE GHOSTS TO REST?

In 1996, Graham Swift's *Last Orders* won the Booker Prize. As I suggested in the last chapter, the novel is a skilful and moving allegory of contemporary life. It borrows from the tradition of the pilgrimage – from Chaucer's *The Canterbury Tales* and Faulkner's *As I Lay Dying* – in its attempt to domesticate, through small narratives, the sublime and *unheimlich* narrative of human mortality: in this way the book is a further indication of Swift's long absorption in the task of doing justice, in fictional form, to history and change in a post-romantic secular world. In this world religion no longer offers universal succour, and neither art nor romantic love seem capable of salving the isolation of the modern hyper-individualised self. One might surmise that the reward of the Booker was a recognition that *Last Orders* had finally solved the problem of aesthetic and cultural coherence – that is, a fit between form, content and context – towards which all Swift's earlier novels have been directed. *Last Orders*, it might be noted, is more wry comedy than tragedy.

In the first part of this chapter I chart Swift's engagement with the movement from a tragic and melancholic romanticism to the human comedy present in the *Last Orders*. In the second half of the chapter I offer a discussion of humour and 'ordered disorder' as ways of circumventing the death drive of the melancholy superego.

Broadly speaking, modernity can be understood as the attempt which began in the sixteenth and seventeenth centuries to understand the world – philosophically and scientifically (the distinction between philosophy and science in the modern sense is, itself, born of modernity) – *without* recourse to a religious or mystical narrative. But, in doing away with God, and in replacing Him with man as the source of all knowledge about the world, modernity opened within itself a sort of abyss of meaninglessness: the joy offered by reason's escape from superstition was accompanied by the particularly modern terror induced by the apprehension of an utterly meaningless world. To put it another way, those human needs and feelings which had been more or less securely held and provided for by religious and traditional narratives of man's meaning and place in the cosmos no longer worked; in their place was something like a conceptual void – an infinitely empty place where God had been.

Of course, Enlightenment science was in many ways very successful in filling out the void which it had created; it offered compelling explanations of the physical laws of the universe and the workings of nature, and many saw (as some still see) God's hand in these. Nonetheless, there was something ruthless and impersonal in this God of physical laws and cause and effect; the mid and late eighteenth-century interest in the category of the sublime testifies to a cultural attempt to name that which had become distant, frightening in its impersonal force, and un-nameable. The definition of the sublime was and is: that vastness which can be *conceived* of, but which defies *representation*. For example, one can grasp the concept of vast numbers, or of infinity, but the mind fails before the task of actually representing these adequately.

Although, by the early decades of the nineteenth century, both philosophical and scientific narratives of modern progress had appeared – whether mechanical, as in the successes of the Industrial Revolution, or philosophical, as in the great synthetic thesis offered by Hegel's *Phenomenology of Spirit* – the nineteenth century remained, largely, culturally anxious and melancholic. That is to say that a great many people worried about the rise of a mechanistic philosophy and attitude to life,[1] and much of the literature and culture of the mid-century and beyond is funereal and preoccupied with the difficulty of encountering mortality and with mourning it.[2]

Baudelaire's perception of the nature of nineteenth-century modernity was that it was essentially funereal. His quest to discover the true 'painter of modern life', who would be capable of representing modernity to itself, in all its fevered and fashionable transience[3], allows us to understand the extent to which the burden of representing the un-nameable – once borne by religious representations (in narratives and visual art) – was transferred, throughout the eighteenth and nineteenth centuries, onto secular art. It is, as Jay Bernstein argues, in art that mourning is to be accomplished (if at all) in the modern world.[4]

SWIFT AND MOURNINGFUL DREAMS

Graham Swift's work offers an exemplary case of the artist who attempts to come to terms with, and to represent, both the possibility and the difficulty of really mourning modernity's losses – the loss of traditional forms of knowledge with the advent of the absolutely *new*, and, as I have said, the loss of the solaces of a personally revealed God. From the first to the last, Swift's novels explore the failure of romantic conceptions of meaningfulness – whether in Hegel's story of history as the gradual unfolding of spiritual knowledge towards the perfect, mutually recognising, community, or in romantic art's conception of aesthetic knowledge as offering a moment of healing transcendence in the mystery of symbolic unity. Somehow, one senses, Swift wants something earthier and more lowly, something closer to the gamble and the muddle and mess.

There are, Freud says, two responses to loss.[5] One is the crazy mourning in which the madness of grief (and it *is* a madness, a form of psychosis) can be gradually transformed into some form of accommodation with reality, and into some kind of renewal of the lifeful forces of eros (or the life drives), against the depradations and compulsive repetitions of entropy which Freud named the death drive.[6] The other response to loss – in which mourning becomes pathological and impossible – Freud called melancholia. In melancholia, loss is perceived not simply as the loss of some other – whether a cherished person or a cherished idea – but, due to the narcissistic incorporation of the object in order to preserve it, it is perceived as *the loss of the self*.[7] In mourning, the bereaved and shattered self learns to let go of what has made its world meaningful, to forgive the lost object for leaving, and to make a different world and future; in melancholia, bereavement consists in *not* letting go, in hanging on to the object by internalising it, and in punishing it for going. Clearly, the structure of melancholia thus consists in forms of self-punishment in which what is nostalgically sought is a past satisfaction, and a sense of wholeness or self-completion in which the cherished object is preserved, rather than a radically changed future in which both self and world are utterly transformed in the castrating experience of permanent loss.

The task which, over his entire *oeuvre*, Swift sets himself is that of discovering how the self-destructive melancholias of modernity can be turned into the healthy mournings of something that we might call postmodernity, understood as a precondition for a *new* modernity. What we call the postmodern seems to consist in the struggle between melancholia and mourning – between, on the one hand, nostalgic turns to the past and a masochistic sense of social fragmentations, and, on the other, the attempt to imagine differently reconstituted communities and selves; we might therefore say that the *outcome* of postmodernity, seen as the attempt to live with loss and uncertainty as a permanent condition, would be the discovery or invention of ways of being in the world which move beyond the harsh individual-

ism of utilitarian modernity, and towards a different way of accounting for and valuing human needs. It is this problem, the problem of
inventing an aesthetic form capable of telling us something about the
invention of new cultural, social and political forms – a '*new* modernity or 'second Enlightenment'[8] – which drives Swift's work.[9] His
central preoccupations lie in the aesthetic imagining of cultural
mourning as a form of erotic (that is to say lifeful and loving) and, in
the end, *communal*, not individualistic, labour in the world. This
would be a sort of *good work* in the world akin to what the philosopher Gillian Rose has called 'love's work'.[10] Swift only finally
achieves this full communality of working voices in *Last Orders*.

Lack of space prevents me from offering detailed readings of all
Swift's six novels; here I will deal, in differing amounts of detail, with
a symptomatic selection beginning with the first, *The Sweet Shop
Owner* (1980), moving to the third, *Waterland* (1983), and concluding with the fifth, *Ever After* (1992).

THE SWEET SHOP OWNER: SWEETS FOR MY SWEET, SUGAR FOR MY HONEY, I'LL NEVER, EVER, LET YOU GO

No reader of Graham Swift will have any difficulty in recognising the
very English nostalgia and melancholy present in his novels. This is
particularly true of his first novel, *The Sweet Shop Owner*. Although
the fictional chronology extends back to 1937, the book is largely
taken up with the careful domestic detailing of South London petty
bourgeois life in the period from World War Two up to 1974.

The Sweet Shop Owner's central character is Willy Chapman, and
he is the first manifestation in novel-length form of what will come to
be a regular theme in Swift's writing, that of the 'weak' (and often
phlegmatic) English father. These 'failed fathers' come to take on an
increasingly obvious allegorical weight in Swift's fiction. They function as signs of the failure of cultural and historical continuity – the
failure, in psychoanalytic terms, of the 'paternal' function of bearing
and transmitting the cultural 'law' – but also, of course, as figures of
a divine Father who no longer 'works'. In *The Sweet Shop Owner*,
the allegorical dimension remains embryonic, however, and it is only
retrospectively – from two or three novels on – that the reader of
Swift's work will be in a position fully to appreciate the significance
of Willy as husband and father as he is inscribed over a series of South
London high street *tableaux* during the course of thirty years.

Willy appears to have no direction or ambition of his own. He represents simply the pattern of order itself – and the pattern of an essentially unreflective English way of life: 'He had planned nothing. Not for himself. And yet he knew: plans emerged. You stepped into them' (SSO, p24). In a larger sense, this pattern, and Willy's unthinking confidence in it, signifies the phlegmatic and domestic conservatism of 'England' – a conservatism palpable in so many of the British films produced during the 1950s. This particular kind of Englishness – a rather phlegmatic and domestic commitment to the sort of order which Alison Light sees being formulated as 'Englishness' during the 1930s,[11] and which is drawn upon, extended and developed by the post-war consensus and the welfare state – is the Englishness from which Swift attempts to break free with *Waterland*. It represents, as does Willy himself, a kind of wilful and conservative blindness to the forces of history and culture, an attendance to the pattern of an eternal present – a 'forever England' – which seeks to hold off change.

The *point* of the novel is to show that Willy's unreflective romanticism – his attempt, in staging his own death, to force the symbolic unity which will be signified by his estranged daughter Dorry's return home on *her* birthday and *his* deathday – does not work. Willy's romantic fantasy is that, with Dorry's response to the nostalgic commitment to return home, the 'pattern' – and historical and cultural transmission – will be assured: 'She would go down, weep, clasp his knees, as though she were clasping the limbs of a cold, stone statue that stares out and beyond without seeing. He would be history' (SSO p10). In the absence of this, all Willy's devotion to maintaining the pattern will, for him, have amounted to nothing, and he will have failed to establish his proper paternal – and one might say, in the psychoanalytic sense, symbolic – relation to history. The novel closes with, precisely, this failure; its failed closure thus inaugurates Swift's search for a form and content capable of giving full expression to a post-romantic, postmodern cultural experience.

For Swift, the transmission of culture (the meaning of history and human creative capacity) is seen as the (symbolic, paternal) task in a modern culture in which the paternal fiction (an authoritative and unifying cultural narrative) no longer has the power to command assent. (Dorry's doctoral thesis is, significantly, on 'Romantic Poetry and the Sense of History' (SSO p216).) Swift thus initially comes at the problem of bourgeois romantic individualism – and the unifying of subjective and objective worlds in a disinterested aesthetic contem-

plation which is 'like' romantic love inasmuch as each seems to overcome alienation – from the point of view of the post-romantic who
clings to the pattern of an idea long after its content has proved to be
insubstantial. In *Waterland*, the paternal task will come to be
presented as overwhelmingly difficult and, formally, Swift's concern
with cultural history and the means for handing it on will move from
the critical vestiges of romantic symbolism towards the complex
layering – and more open-ended – form of allegory.

WATERLAND: LETTING GO OF THE SAVIOUR OF THE WORLD

The North Cambridgeshire Fens are not the first place which springs
to mind when one thinks of 'Englishness'; they are decidedly
unpretty. Swift's imaginary Fenland town of Gildsey is, however,
umbilically tied to Greenwich (and England in all its imperial splen-
dour) by the line of 0 degrees longitude which passes through both.
The homeland imagined here is both something and nothing, and the
landscape of the Fens is, appropriately, sublime. Not only is it a vast
flatness where the light of an extensive sky drowns all other scales,
but its very contourlessness drives men beyond reason: 'To live in the
Fens is to receive strong doses of reality. The great, flat monotony of
reality; the wide empty space of reality. Melancholia and self-murder
are not unknown in the Fens. Heavy drinking, madness and sudden
acts of violence are not uncommon. How do you surmount reality,
children?' (WL p15).

Waterland's narrator, Tom Crick, is fifty-three, lives in Greenwich
and is a history teacher in a local South London comprehensive. His
A level class on the French Revolution is interrupted by Price – a
student who can see no use in History because knowing how things
have been in the past makes no difference to how things are in the
present or will be in the future:

> Children, it was one of your number, a curly-haired boy called Price,
> in the habit (contrary to regulations but passed over by me) of daubing
> his cheeks with an off-white make-up which gave to his face the pallor
> of a corpse, who once, interrupting the French Revolution and voicing
> the familiar protest that every history teacher learns to expect (what is
> the point, use, need, etc., of History), asserted roundly that history was
> 'a fairy-tale'.

(A teacher-baiter. A lesson-spoiler. Every class has to have one. But this one's different ...)

What matters,' he went on, not knowing what sort of fairy-tale was about to envelop both his history teacher and his history teacher's wife, 'is the here and now. Not the past. The here and now and the future.' (The very sentiments, Price – but you didn't see that – of 1789.) And then – alluding rapidly to certain topics of the day (the Afghan crisis, the Tehran hostages, the perilous and apparently unhaltable build-up of nuclear arms) and drawing from you, his class-mates, a sudden and appalling venting of your collective nightmares – he announced, with a trembling lip that was not just the result of uttering words that must have been (true, Price?) carefully rehearsed: 'The only important thing ...'

'Yes, Price – the only important thing – ?'

'The only important thing about history, I think, sir, is that it's got to the point where it's probably about to end.'

So we closed our textbooks. Put aside the French Revolution. So we said goodbye to that old and hackneyed fairy-tale with its Rights of Man, liberty caps, cockades, tricolours, not to mention its hissing guil-lotines, and its quaint notion that it had bestowed on the world a New Beginning.

I began, having recognised in my young but by no means carefree class the contagious symptoms of fear: 'Once upon a time ...' (WL p6)

The fairy-tale Crick tells, which 'like ... all good fairy-tales' must have a setting which is 'both palpable and unreal' (WL p6) is of the Fens. Tom is faced with redundancy in a Thatcherite Britain dedi-cated to the most superficial utilitarianism: 'We're cutting back on history ...You know how the cuts are biting. And you know the kind of pressure I'm under – "practical relevance to today's real world" – that's what they're demanding' (WL p19). He is also faced with a mad wife who is driven to stealing a baby from the local Safeways to replace the child she could never conceive following a teenage abor-tion in 1943, and with a class of fearful eighteen year olds. His response is to turn away from the 'grand Narrative' (WL p53) of History – which tells everything on a grand public scale but explains nothing of intimate experience – and to begin to recount the small tale of his own family origins.

The 'fairy-story' of the Fens, and of Tom Crick's family, is offered as an allegory of the French Revolution's tale of the ways in which 'progress' can lead to terror. The Revolution itself stands as a sort of synecdoche of Enlightenment Modernity, and of a false notion of progress. Tom's story is a sustained critique of Price's belief that something sublime called 'the here and now' ('which brings both joy and terror' (WL p52)) can ever be grasped. The here and now in Tom's tale is pure event – a reality of such immediacy as to be, strictly speaking, intolerable – and a thing which, unless tamed by narratives, drives people mad. Crick's story does not give up on the idea of progress, but it offers a different model for thinking the 'here and now' (necessary but impossible), and a different goal (allegorised in the idea of siltation and reclamation) for historical, philosophical, political (and, implicitly, literary) narratives.

The novel is delivered as a series of 'lessons' to Crick's class. Each 'lesson' has to be read – like sediments of silt – allegorically against all the others; with an archaeology and genealogy of meaning building up as the story, of land and family, progresses. In chapter 3 – 'About the Fens' – the reader learns that the history of the reclamation of the Fens from the watery reaches of the North Sea in the mid-seventeenth century is congruent with the rise and consolidation of early entrepreneurial capitalism in England. Whilst the paternal Cricks acquire the English virtue of phlegm – and 'outwit reality' by telling stories (WL p15) – the maternal Atkinsons outwit reality by acquiring Ideas and Land: 'While the Atkinsons made history, the Cricks spun yarns' (WL p15).

One of the meanings of the domestication of the Fens is thus to offer an allegory of modern development, and of the modern 'English' character, as both entrepreneurial and phlegmatic. But, 'The Fens were formed by silt. Silt: a word which when you utter it, letting the air slip thinly between your teeth, invokes a slow, sly, insinuating agency. Silt: which shapes and undermines continents; which demolishes as it builds; which is simultaneous accretion and erosion; neither progress nor decay' (WL p7). Undermining their first meaning, the Fens (and capitalist progress and pragmatic 'English' identity) now become less substantial: 'The chief fact about the Fens is that they are reclaimed land, land that was once water, and which, even today, is not quite solid' (WL p7). 'The Fens are still being reclaimed even to this day. Strictly speaking they are never reclaimed, only being reclaimed' (WL p8).

The story of *Waterland* concerns the local and domestic causes and effects of the murder by violence and then drowning, in the summer of 1943, of the adolescent Tom Crick's friend Freddie Parr.

Uncovering the meaning of the (unrecognised) murder – the coroner's verdict was 'Accidental Death' – means uncovering the history of the Cricks and Atkinsons and their various historical relationships to the Fens. It also means uncovering the present meaning of Mary Crick's descent into madness – overwhelmed, as she is, by the 'here and now'. These little local histories, intimately tied to the history of the Fens, are offered as an allegory of the transformation of a sublimely ungraspable 'nothing' into the 'something' of the everyday – as ways of making the vast Nothing of the Fens into a local and knowable something, and, also, as a way of quelling the 'restless thoughts' of Tom's frightened 'children' (WL p6).

The Atkinsons are brewers. In the course of their business they cause canals to be built and ditches to be drained, all of which must be regulated by locks and dredged of silt. These latter tasks fall to the Cricks. While the Cricks labour, phlegmatically, at the business of keeping the Fenland solid, and of tending – via locks and stories – to the symbolic limits which must be set upon a maddening nothingness, the Atkinsons – ever entrepreneurially attentive to desire – labour at the business of providing it, overwhelmingly, with an undermining and dissolving liquor. The story of the Fens, and the Atkinsons and Cricks, is, then, the story of a history which is also a 'fairy tale' – a many-layered allegory which formally enacts its own thesis concerning the impossibility of keeping things (land, water; truth, fiction; something, nothing) separate.

Initially drawn to History because it seems to offer real answers, Tom Crick gradually comes to understand that History is not reality, and that reality is sublime. History is the sense we make of the stark and terrifying reality which always threatens to escape our orderings: 'Reality's not strange, not unexpected. Reality doesn't reside in the sudden hallucination of events. Reality is uneventfulness, vacancy, flatness. Reality is that nothing happens ... I present to you History, the fabrication, the diversion, the reality-obscuring drama. History and its near relative Histrionics ...' (WL p34). All we have are 'stories' in which each actor, even if he has missed 'the grand repertoire of history' imitates, in miniature, 'its longing for presence, for feature, for purpose, for content' (WL pp34-5).

Significantly, in the light of Swift's earlier work, the drama of the murder-mystery story in *Waterland* centres on a series of misconceptions about the meaning of love. Following the burning down of the Atkinson brewery at Gildsey in a night of riotous and carnivalesque drunkenness (the result of a particularly sublime Coronation ale brewed by Ernest Atkinson and later bequeathed to his son Dick) in 1911, Tom's maternal grandfather, Ernest – convinced that there will be war and that the world will be visited by unprecedented calamity – withdraws with his daughter Helen (the only 'left-over fragment of paradise' (WL p189)) to the isolation of Kessling Hall where, in 1915, because they love each other, father and daughter enter upon an incestuous relationship.

After the Great War, the hall is turned – at Helen's suggestion and in order to distract her father from his increasing desire for a son from her who will be 'the Saviour of the World' – into a home for shell-shocked soldiers. It is here, in 1922, that Helen meets Tom's father, Henry Crick, and that they fall in love. Henry's old Fenlander capacity for telling stories has been shattered by the experience of war ('He thinks: there is only reality, there are no stories left' (WL p17)), but gradually love and stories from Helen restore him to health, memory, narrative and home. The second love replacing the first, Helen sees in this the opportunity to assuage her father's desire and also to set herself free. She agrees to become pregnant by her father provided that Ernest consents to her marriage to Henry. This accomplished, Helen – settled with Henry at the lock-keeper's cottage on the Atkinson Lock – gives birth in March 1923 to Tom's elder (half) brother, Dick. But the saviour of the world turns out to be 'a potato head' (WL p200), a 'natural' who, although sometimes giving the impression of being a Holy Fool looking down in 'lofty and lucid mindlessness, half in contempt and half in pity at a world blinded by its own glut of imagination', is 'irreclaimable' (WL p32).

Dick, always smelling of silt, is a monstrous personification of the resistant sublimity of the Fens. Of appropriately prodigious (not to say sublime) phallic proportions, he is a figuration of the will to seize hold of reality and to 'save the world'. Described as a half fish, half man (WL pp165 and 309) – at home on land or in water and capable of remaining submerged for an uncanny length of time – Dick is the vacant-faced 'here and now' made flesh: 'Not a saviour of the world. A potato-head. Not a hope for the future. A Numbskull with the dull, vacant stare of a fish' (WL p209). As the murderer – whose weapon is a bottle of the ale of 1911 bequeathed by his father/grandfather – Dick is the 'nothing' *grounds* of the history – the story – which follows. Nevertheless he cannot become a *part* of history. He is the sublime 'reality' upon which History is acted out. Himself the result of an culturally unbinding act, Dick cannot understand 'love' – which is a form of historical binding-up – and have babies and, in the end, he must be returned to the sublime and watery nothingness from which, symbolically, he emerged.

Ernest Atkinson is the most desperate and vivid example yet of Swift's many troubled fathers. His attempt to father a new saviour out of the paradise of Helen is 'like tying up into a knot the thread that runs into the future, it's like a stream wanting to flow backwards' (WL p197). Its result – Dick – has all the vacant sublimity of the Fenland silt with which he is continually associated. Dick's conception, and his association with nature and silt, mark him out as yet another symbol of failed love in Swift's work: 'Love. Lu-love. Lu-lu-love. Does it ward off evil? Will its magic word suspend indefinitely the link between cause and effect?' (WL p259). Love, for Swift, and along with art as the telling of stories, is what humans do to ward off the fearful sublimity of natural existence. It is because he does not understand the complexity of narratives and love (is, himself, the unwitting result of over-complex love), and childishly confuses the latter with making babies (which, because of the size of his penis, he also cannot do), that – 'loving' Mary Metcalfe (Mrs Tom Crick-to-be) and believing Tom's story that Freddie Parr is the father of the baby which Mary and Tom have conceived – Dick murders Freddie. When Tom tells Dick the truth, and also tells him why he must not have babies, Dick – in a self-sacrificing parody of the redemptive Christian act – throws himself into the River Ouse: 'He's on his way. Obeying instinct. Returning. The Ouse flows to the sea ...' (WL p310).

Mary Crick's 'problem' is not so much her belief in the fiction of a saviour, and a new beginning, as her inability to turn her fascination with the sublime here and now (a happening in the face of nothing, a prodigiously sized and fascinating phallus which is 'too big') into a narrative:

> First there is nothing; then there is happening; a state of emergency. And after the happening, only the telling of it. But sometimes the happening won't stop and let itself be turned into memory. So she's still in the midst of events (a supermarket adventure, something in her arms, a courtroom in which she proclaims in a loud and clear voice: 'God told') which have not ceased. Which is why it's impossible to get through. Which is why she cannot cross into the safe, sane realm of hindsight and answer the questions of the white-coated doctors: 'Now tell us, Mrs Crick, you can tell us everything, you can tell ...' (WL p284).

The story (as opposed to the novel) ends with Tom Crick's valedictory address to his school. Contained in chapter 49 – 'About Empire Building' – his speech addresses both the fantasy of the paternal fiction (killing bad fathers and needing better ones) and, not for the first time, the 'fiction' of modernity as a New Beginning. In place of these, Crick offers history and progress according to the model of the *reclamation* of the Fens: 'My humble model for progress is the reclamation of land. Which is repeatedly, never-endingly retrieving what is lost. A dogged and vigilant business. A dull yet valuable business. A hard, inglorious business. But you shouldn't go mistaking the reclamation of land for the building of empires' (WL p291).

BUT IF I LET GO FOR *EVER AFTER*, HOW CAN I TAKE MY LIFE?

Ever After is a novel very much concerned with different kinds of loss, with mourning, and with coming to terms with grief – with all its 'simulations, fabrications, biographical conjurations ... the ... wilder delusions, the subterfuges, superstitions of grief' (EA p255).

William Unwin was once an academic, a lecturer in English, and then, later, the manager of his successful actress wife Ruth Vaughan. Following her death from cancer some eighteen months before the time of the narrative, Bill, paralysed with grief, is 'appointed' to the Ellison Fellowship at a Cambridge college. The Fellowship has been endowed by Bill's American stepfather, 'Uncle Sam' Ellison, from the fortune amassed from his plastics business, on the discreet understanding that Bill will be its first beneficiary. Appropriately to the conventions of its elegiac form, the story is narrated from the pastoral setting of the Fellows' Garden during the long vacation where Bill sits – invalid-like – recovering from the suicide attempt he made three weeks earlier, some twelve-odd months after his appointment.

What Bill is supposed to be doing with his Fellowship is writing a book based around the mid-nineteenth-century notebooks of a distant maternal relative – Matthew Pearce – which came into his hands on the death of his mother nine months earlier. The notebooks, written intermittently over a six year period from 1854 to 1860, concern Matthew's gradual loss of faith following the death of his third child, Felix (happiness), at the age of two. In an entry dated 10th June 1854, Matthews cites the earlier moment of doubt which the child's death now recalls for him: how, while holidaying in Lyme

Regis some ten years earlier, before his marriage, he stumbled across the fossil remains of an ichthyosaur, and, in that moment, had some intimation that Man is not the central purpose of God's creation; that human life, if it has any purpose at all, might be more a question of experiment.

Matthew's story is that of a young man who, emerging from three years at Oxford in 1840 to enter a career as a surveyor, remains entirely convinced of the literal truth of the Bible as a foundation of meaning. 'It meant that the profounder questions of existence were settled and one was free to go out on to the surface of the world and do good, practical work. And the surface of the world only brought you back to the central fact: nature's handiwork, and man's too, since it exploited the unchanging laws that were part of nature's design, was evidence of God's' (EA p92). But the ichthyosaur fossil, Felix's death and, finally, the publication of Darwin's *Origin of Species* in 1859 chip away at this certainty, and bring him to believe, in the end, that there might indeed be no God at all but only an endless series of evolutionary struggles.

Using the 'original data' of the Pearce notebooks, Bill Unwin intends to make this account of mid-nineteenth-century loss of faith the subject of his Fellowship research. Instead, what Unwin actually writes is the story of his own life and loss. The two stories – both telling of the vertiginous experience of stumbling upon the sublime 'real' in all its appalling resistance and nauseating emptiness – thus resonate across each other, one from an entirely domestic space, with the experience of losing a cherished wife, and the other positioned within a much bigger cultural crisis: the experience of modernity as a huge collective confrontation with the loss of faith.

Both Bill Unwin and the ancient university where he now resides – and which was once supposed to be the defender of authentic civilised values and Enlightenment, 'rising like some fantastical lantern out of the miasmal fens and out of the darkness of dark ages' (EA p9) – now owe their existence, in part, to that apparently most inauthentic (because entirely imitative) of things: plastic. Plastic is a substitute for the real stuff. But, insists Bill's 'Uncle Sam', 'the real stuff is running out, it's used up, it's blown away, or it costs too much. You gotta have substitoots' (EA p7).

The university, once the site of 'the true, real, permanent thing' is now 'artificial and implausible, like a painstakingly contrived film set'. For Bill what is 'real' is what lies beyond the university, and yet that 'real world' is falling apart: 'its social fabric is in tatters, its eco-system is near collapse. Real: that is, flimsy, perishing, stricken, doomed' (EA p2). But most significantly, the 'real stuff' which Unwin believed he had – his love for his actress wife Ruth – is also made of endless fabrications: the fabrications of art and of human love. In his function as a college tutor (at least up to the point when he discovers the truth of his *real* paternity, that he is the son of a nameless engine driver on Brunel's Great Western railway which, surveyed by Matthew Pearce in the mid-nineteenth century, was the site of Bill's own 'Freudian' train-spotting and 'paternal' identifications in the mid-twentieth century[12]), Bill remains unfashionably committed to the notion that literature is good because it is 'beautiful', because it transforms the everyday into the sublime ('A great deal of literature is only (only!) the obvious transformed into the sublime' (EA p70)), and thus provides access to an intimation of, a moment of stumbling upon – albeit retrospectively – the truth of reality. But with Ruth's death, it is, indeed, the 'commonplace' obviousness of the real – the real in all its vulgar everydayness – which Bill faces. ('And nothing is left but this impossible absence. This space at your side the size of a woman, the size of a life, the size – of the world. Ah yes, the monstrosity, the iniquity of love – that another person should *be* the world. What does it matter if the world (out there) is lost, doomed, if there is no sense of purpose, rhyme or reason to the schemeless scheme of things, so long as – But when she is gone, you indict the universe' (EA p256)).

In *Ever After*, the quest for the father, and his truth, is finally abandoned. What moves to the fore in its place (the 'inauthentic' place of 'ever after') is the question of how adequately to symbolise the loss itself. In other words, Swift's question increasingly becomes one which is concerned with the relationship between aesthetic form and ethical content. The form must be one which is capable of symbolising the trauma of loss. As Uncle Sam says 'You gotta have substitoots' (EA p7). Indeed, as Peter Sacks points out, the work of elegy is precisely that of the substitution of the melancholic's narcissism by the processes of symbolisation: 'primary desire never attains its literal objective except in death, or in a deathlike loss of identity. The only object that such a desire can possess in life will be a sign or substitute for what it cannot have'.[13] That the language of substitution should issue from such a source (the resonantly named 'Uncle Sam' fulfils the role of Claudius in Bill's identification with Hamlet) merely lends strength to Sacks's contention that elegy stages a work of mourning which attempts to recapitulate the resolution to the oedipal drama.

Bill's story is of a father who kills himself – apparently because of his wife's adultery with the young Sam Ellison – in 1945 when Bill was nine years old. Bill identifies himself, oedipally, with the melancholic Hamlet. His dilemma is to be 'actuated, or immobilised, by two questions: 1) is there or is there not any point to it all? 2) Shall I kill Claudius? Or to put it another way: shall I kill Claudius or shall I kill myself?' (EA p5) In other words, the symbolic value of the father's bequest lies not in his life – in which he is simply immediate authority – but in his death, his murder, with which symbolic transformation, mediation and exchange becomes possible. Bill's life is dominated by his mother's seductiveness and his father's death, by understanding the cause and meaning of the latter, and by his unfulfilled desire for revenge upon Sam.

In the end, however, Bill gives up on the melancholic's desire for revenge. It isn't, finally, what matters:

> I read up on Brunel; but I do not research my own father. I summon up Matthew, but I do not try to know my own father. My nameless, engine-driving, killed-in-the-war father. And why should I when I never got to know the living, breathing man whom I took to be -? What difference does it make? The true or the false. This one or that one. The world will not shatter because of a single – misconception ... (EA p204)

The novel's concluding chapter opens with an ambivalent restatement of the above theme – this time in a way which also refers the reader back to the famous oedipal ambivalence of Hamlet: 'It's not the end of the world. It is. Life goes on. It doesn't. Why seems it so particular with thee?' (EA p249). And it is precisely this ambivalence (as in the novel's concluding sentence) associated with art which, as it were, resolves by not resolving.

So, what kind of allegorical 'solution' does Swift, via Bill Unwin's story, offer? The novel closes with a return and a repetition. In the final chapter Bill remembers the carefully planned occasion of the first time he and Ruth made love and – nakedly – presented themselves and their lives to each other. Bill tells Ruth what he has never told anyone – that his father killed himself – and remembers 'how strange, how incomprehensible ... How unreal' (EA p261) the phrase sounded then to two young people in love. The novel ends with 'How impossible that either of these young people, whose lives, this night, have never been so richly possessed, so richly embraced, will ever come to such a pass. He took his life, he took his life' (EA p261).

The final sentence is deeply ambiguous. Does the pronoun refer to the father or to the son, or to both, and in which phrase? The repetition and the content suggest, once more, the re-emergence of the double (Bill Unwin is, after all, his own 'plastic' imitation) with which the novel opens, and this directs us towards the repetitions and uncanniness of the death drive which lies behind and beyond the pleasure principle motivating the lovers. Another reading is possible, however, in which the deathly sense of the verb is read erotically – as, indeed, Bill and Ruth have just taken each other. In this sense 'he took his life' signifies acceptance of life as it is – both terrible and banal, sublime and domestic, at the same time – rather than suicide. This semantic ambiguity, a sort of agreement not to close off, or possess, the meaning of the object (in *this* case, the novel), suggests a desire to tolerate anxiety and ambivalence, which is a part of the relinquishment of narcissistic melancholias. But the move from the narcissisms of the child to the sociality of the adult consciousness involves labour and community with others in the world. As I argued in the previous chapter, it is to these themes that Swift turns in *Last Orders*.

FRAGMENTATIONS: MODERNIST *JOUISSANCE* AS BOREDOM

As Patricia Waugh's *Harvest of the Sixties* demonstrates, the word which most adequately describes the period from the 1960s to the 1990s is 'fragmentation'.[14] Waugh's text is a comprehensive litany of all the sources – critical, creative, and political – through which this experience has been articulated in the second half of the twentieth century. To read about – let alone seriously to think about – this period is to encounter (provided one remains committed to the idea of human attachments and goods) some element of the sublime. That Western cultures are in trouble is a commonplace to be found in any newspaper every day of the week. All boundaries and distinctions other than the grossly materialistic seem gone or tenuous. As in Steven Spielberg's *Poltergeist* (dir. Tobe Hooper, 1982), a terrifying uncanniness roars through the cracks of doors *inside* the house to suck us into some God-knows-where oblivion whose only familiar locus appears to be the television set. Like the site of literal alienation in James Cameron's *Aliens* (1986), the sublime is figured as vaginal or womblike – a site of narcissistic engulfment – but, in both films, the redeemer of the child is not the father but the mother. As I have already argued, this shift from a redeeming father to a redeeming mother is a significant feature of contemporary cultural imaginings – one only finally achieved by Swift in the character of Ame in *Last Orders*. There, the cultural continuity traditionally, and in Freudian vein, associated with the father's commanding injunction (the 'castrative No') to renounce primary narcissism, is borne, instead, by the mother. It is Amy who 'remembers', and tends the link between past and future in her weekly visits to her idiot daughter June. It is Amy who bears witness to the present, no matter how 'idiotic', as the continuity of debts and promises passed on. Where, in *The Sweet Shop Owner*, Willy Chapman's 'relay' fails because its aim is death, Amy's succeeds because its aim is life – no matter how seemingly stupid. The difference between the labour of Willy, racing, and the much slower labour of Ame, is that one depends upon the fantasy of a finally triumphant, romantic closure, the other upon the reality of the lesser, stoical or faithful, goal of an open-ended continuing. In *Last Orders*, the pilgrims, especially the 'little Ray of Hope', understand the virtue of continuing with the risk and gamble of life. Very different from the fixity of Willy's experience of community, this is mourning as mutuality and acceptance of change. As in Rose's reading of 'Gathering the Ashes of Phocion', the tone of ethical responsibility which determines the men's pilgrimage in *Last Orders*, is set by a woman and mother, not by a father.

A sense of boundary-loss is extremely unsettling; when everything is the same, when there is no sense of difference, one confronts the repetition of the death drive: in death *there is nowhere else to go*. This is the hopelessness and terror invoked by sublimity. 'The dead', says undertaker Vic in Graham Swift's *Last Orders*, 'are all the same'; and in Anthony Minghella's film *Truly, Madly, Deeply* (1990), the greatest sense of uncanniness is produced by the sameness, and the same boredom, of the dead who crowd into the melancholic central character's house after the death of her husband. Once arrived, they do nothing except watch old films; their ennui is overpowering; one senses even the effort it takes to haunt someone back to life with your boredom – which is the ghostly husband's finally successful aim.

In fact, it would of course be truer to say that boredom is a response rather than a quality. People who are boring are not themselves necessarily bored. Boredom, as Winnicott once intimated, is a response to something unbearable; boredom is a defence against something one wishes to avoid – in oneself or in the other.[15] Inexplicable boredom with someone else, Winnicott implies, is very often a defence against psychical illness in them, or, a defence against the perception that someone's proper affective life is absent. This experience of an absence of affect in the other signals the presence of a 'False Self'. In other words, what one defends against is the inhumanity of the other, the fragmentations of the death drive in them, and the boredom of the dead.

The sublime – whether as terror, banality, or boredom – is the categorisation of the inhuman which accompanies modernity. Its dimension is the massive: the masses; mass production; mass consumption; mass destruction; mass culture; mass communication; and anything which can be spoken about but never wholly represented. In Britain and the United States, in the 1970s and 1980s, massification invaded critical thought, and melancholic philosophies with the fragmenting drive of *laissez-faire* capitalism became attached to revolutionary marxist critiques of 'bourgeois realism'. In *S/Z* (1973) Roland Barthes celebrated the 'writerly' text as a form of anti-realist *jouissance* in which reading and *jouissance* were akin to boredom. The writerly text is 'the text that imposes a state of loss, that discomforts (perhaps to the point of a certain boredom), unsettles the reader's historical, cultural, psychological assumptions, the consistency of his tastes, values, memories, brings to a crisis his relation with language'.[16] Anglo-American cultures perhaps received this and other post-structuralist avant-gardisms too literally. Nonetheless, it is significant and symptomatic that it was in the countries where liberalism (and its crisis) were most entrenched that the essentially psychotic celebration of fragmentation, death-like *jouissance*, and an 'I' which is 'spoken from elsewhere' took firmest canonical hold. This is, as it were, a post-structuralist theoretical formulation of Winnicott's False Self. The latter is a defence against annihilation;[17] but while the 'post-structuralist' formulation may be descriptively accurate of the condition of being a normative subject in modernity (a topic dealt with in chapter 2), the theory offers nothing equivalent to Winnicott's True Self. The post-structuralist prescription to celebrate such a condition – a sort of radical splitting of mania and depression akin to alternating between dancing on one's own grave and lying on it in a state of exquisite ennui – is a weak and dangerous response to despair.

At best, the nihilism and wilful difficulty of the kinds of philosophical and critical languages deployed during the 1970s and 1980s (and, by some, in the 1990s) can perhaps be understood as avant-garde (or, at worst, parodic avant-garde) attempts to figure the unfigurable sublimity of the times. Terry Eagleton believes postmodernism to be a parody of avant-gardism: 'It is as though postmodernism represents the cynical belated revenge wreaked by bourgeois culture upon its revolutionary antagonists'.[18]

NEW AGE AND CARNIVAL

Another, largely non-academic, version of bourgeois self-subversion is met in the 1960s and post-1960s phenomenon which is now termed 'the New Age'. If post-structuralist forms of postmodernism celebrated the fragmenting of texts and bodies, and sought to deconstruct the powerful (and gendered) oppositions upon which Enlightenment modernity erected its self-understandings, it is, interestingly, the non-academic New Age 'critique' of Enlightenment rationality that is in many ways closer to the powerful scientific critiques of these dualisms (discussed in chapter 5) which have emerged in recent years.

One of the things which is characteristic of post-war, New Age, postmodern thought is the rejection of the form of rationality associated with Enlightenment modernity. As Paul Heelas notes, New Agers share modernity's commitment to a form of utopian vision and, in some cases, its commitment to science (albeit the sort of science – such as chaos theory – which appears to challenge positivistic ways of thinking).[19] Also many aspects of the New Age movement are not inimical to the pleasures of the world, to profit, and to what Heelas calls 'spiritual capitalism'.[20] In spite of some continuities with philosophical and liberal capitalist modernity, the most striking discontinuities concern the New Age rejections of rationality (which are usually referred to as 'ego-operations') and of theism. In Heelas's view, New Agers would find themselves in agreement with the Kantian Enlightenment imperative to self-responsibility and self-knowledge, but they part company with Kant where the Enlightenment version of rationality is concerned.[21] The various doctrines and therapies associated with the New Age tend to be characterised by forms of affective gentleness. In alternative medical treatments, for example, the patient is treated as a whole person, body and soul, whose feelings are important, and the therapist is required to be in touch with his or her feelings when prescribing and healing. Generally speaking, the emphasis seems to be on feeling your way towards self-knowledge (hence the attraction of Eastern religions for New Agers); and a certain kind of cold 'scientific' rationality is viewed as a sort of violence. Animal Rights activists who focus with such passion on scientific 'violence' towards animals are, in a sense, acting out one of the central metaphors of New Age beliefs: that Enlightenment modernity and the forms of reasoning which accompany it as a cultural dominant (bureaucratic and techo-scientific rationalisation; changes in time-consciousness) enact a kind of violence upon the very humanity of human beings. One might say that, in the creation of institutions and other forms of power which are heartless, but with which modern individuals are obliged to comply, New Agers see a version of the 'As if's' and 'False Selves' noted by psychoanalysts. New Age practices seem directed not so much to getting rid of the institutional forms within capitalist societies as to changing them. I will be returning to this argument in chapter 5, but, for the moment, I want simply to note that, viewed in this way, part of the spirit of the New Age can be interpreted as willing forms and practices rather more like the Winnicottian mother than the Freudian father. It is the element of creative play which appears to be being sought here. The father's discipline – especially as played out on a vast scale across modern institutions – seems to produce Schreber-like machines for constraining people. And this aspect of disciplinary power, as Santner argued, leads to an aberrant productivity: the attempt to impose too much order on the world is, from a human point of view, itself disordered.

To return momentarily to Swift's *Waterland* – Ernest Atkinson's dream of a new world order produces Dick, but it also produces another kind of disorder, the Coronation Ale of 1911 and the night of carnival at Gildsey, which, rather than being *simply* deathly, also contains the seeds of renewal. Subverting order, carnival is akin to revolution – it is a time of ferment – but in holding the creative ferment within certain bounds (originally the religious holiday), carnival makes renewal possible.[22] One might paraphrase the psychoanalyst Adam Phillips on the virtues of clutter (discussed later in this chapter) by saying that the kind of 'undoing' associated with the carnivalesque is an undoing which may make it possible to do up something else.

As carnival suggests, subversion, confusion and disorder are closely linked to laughter. In what follows, I want to discuss not the absolute disorder hiding behind compulsive ordering (repetition compulsion), but the sort of disorder and confusion which, held within a larger order, is the source of invention and creativity, and the self- and world-renewal which is mourning, generally. Once again we are entering versions of Winnicottian transitional space, or Hélène Cixous's 'realm of the gift' which she opposes to the calculating, 'male' 'realm of *le propre*'.[23] This space is inhabited by the creativity of ordered disorder, and also by the sequence of disordering and reordering which is involved in humour and in what Freud calls the wit-work or joke-work.[24] This work consists of finding ways in which the death drive and the super-ego can be negotiated and denuded of the harshness which Freud saw as such a destructive component of civilisation. Winnicott himself conceived of this healthy staging of ordered disorder in terms of the music hall:

> It should be possible to link the lessening of omnipotent manipulation and of control and of devaluation to normality, and to a degree of manic defence that is employed by all in everyday life. For instance, one is at a music-hall and on to the stage come the dancers, trained to liveliness. One can say that here is the primal scene, here is exhibition-ism, here is anal control, here is a masochistic submission to discipline, here is a defiance of the super-ego. Sooner or later one adds: here is LIFE. Might it not be that the main point of the performance is a denial of deadness, a defence against depressive 'death inside' ideas, the sexu-alization being secondary.[25]

In his commentary, Adam Phillips notes that 'Winnicott is saying here that a performance could be valuable *because* it was a denial of deadness'.[26]

There are clearly similarities between performance, wit-work and therapeutic work; it may well be the case that this different sense of a 'work' to be done, akin to older religious senses of work on the soul, and most certainly *not* the soulless or soul-selling work associated with selling one's labour as a commodity, is a central feature of the New Age Movement too. Certainly some parts of the movement – most noticably those influenced by the teaching of Gurdjieff – do seem to have this sense in mind when they refer to their task as 'The Work'.[27]

Wit, Freud says, saves us energy when it makes us shoot from one thing to make an unexpected connection with another. The difference between the saving of energy involved in order, and the saving of energy involved in the intentional disorderliness of wit, is that in the first case we save it up and keep on doing it, so that pleasure is almost endlessly deferred; but in the case of wit we spend it immediately as laughter or applause. Above all other forms of entertainment, the joke is absolutely intolerant of the compulsion to repeat: a fact which children only slowly learn.

During 1995 and 1996, the *Guardian* Diary ran a 'Spot the New Order' theme. Its find on 12 January 1996 was something at the BBC rumoured to be called the Efficiency Vision Office. Evidently, the Diary was unable to confirm the existence of this new Birtean device, but it reported a 'distinguished BBC TV presenter' as wearily sighing, 'It's news to me, but it sounds like the usual sort of bollocks. Nothing would surprise me anymore. Nothing.' From the late 1980s on, we have all become familiar, I think, with both this compulsive, contemporary impulse to over-ordering found in public-sector institutions, and also with the weary and sometimes comical response. The TV presenter's comment makes us smile because he is 'distinguished' but brought low – in terms of morale, language and anatomy – in a truly carnivalesque spirit of comic inversion. We identify with the presenter as a thoughtful human being at the mercy of a great, mindless, ordering machine: we jump through its hoops because we are obliged to, like automatic fools. This is the comedy of what Bergson called the '*mécanisation de la vie*': living human beings made to behave like machines. Freud quotes Bergson as saying: 'What is living should never, according to our expectation, be repeated exactly the same. When we find such a repetition we always suspect some mechanism lying behind the living thing'.[28] The *Guardian* Diary shows its comic side; but, of course, we see its tragedy too. In other circumstances – where the confusion between human and automaton, person and machine, is not resolved – the experience is no longer funny, but uncanny and frightening – as in Hoffman's *The Sandman*, or, more recently, in cyborg and replicant films such as the *Terminator* and *Alien* series. Although we no longer live in the machine age of heavy industry and Fordist production, Carlyle's 1829 prophesy of a culture psychically internalising the regularity, predictability and efficiency of machine-perfect production seems to have been met. Like a sliver of ice, the ethos of machine-like efficiency seems to have entered our hearts.

'The joke, or wit, is', Freud says, 'the contribution made to the comic from the realm of the unconscious'.[29] The importance of the joke – in the realm of comic and cosmic laughter – is, in effect, that it allows us to evade the draining and deathly economy of the superego: 'the joke *will evade restrictions and open sources of pleasure that have become inaccessible.*'[30] Wit allows a modern, civilised person to evade the deathliness and repetition compulsion of the superego with its constant demand for order, and allows us to refind the barbaric in ordinary, everyday ways. When we are witty or witting, we make a preposterous saving of meanings, and are able to spend it, without dignity or reserve, in the apparent worthlessness of laughter. What is incalculable, or apparently worthless – messiness, disorder, laughter and tears – *does* have value. This value is political, ethical and aesthetic because it is on the side of life, not death. Humour, we often say, is a pure gift.

Arthur Koestler's *The Act of Creation* (1964) argued that both humour and creativity consist in the thinking together of two apparently incompatible discourses or paradigms:

> The history of science abounds with examples of discoveries greeted with howls of laughter because they seemed to be a marriage of incompatibles – until the marriage bore fruit and the alleged incompatibility turned out to derive from prejudice. The humorist, on the other hand, deliberately chooses discordant codes of behaviour or universes of discourse to expose their hidden incongruities in the resulting clash. Comic discovery is paradox stated – scientific discovery is paradox resolved.[31]

This leads Koestler to go on to point to the necessity of a certain disorderliness within order. Thus, whilst 'Habits are the indispensable core of stability and ordered behaviour' their tendency (echoing Carlyle) is to 'mechanise' and to make men 'automatons'. The creative act, however, 'by connecting previously unrelated dimensions of experience' is 'an act of liberation – the defeat of habit by originality.'[32] Moreover, such originality does not proceed from the stately planned and logical progress through conscious ideas, but from unlooked-for and 'irrational' moments of inspirational incongruity:

> Max Planck, the father of quantum theory, wrote in his autobiography that the pioneer scientist must have 'a vivid intuitive imagination for new ideas not generated by deduction, but by *artistically* creative imagination' ... The quotations could be continued indefinitely, yet I cannot recall any explicit statement to the contrary by eminent mathematician or physicist.

Here then is the apparent paradox. A branch of knowledge which operates predominantly with abstract symbols, whose entire rationale and credo are objectivity, verifiability, logicality, turns out to be dependent on mental processes which are subjective, irrational, and verifiable only after the event.[33]

ORDERLY DISORDER: THE STIMULUS OF A LITTLE CONFUSION

At the beginning of his essay on Amsterdam and Los Angeles, Ed Soja, author of *Postmodern Geography* amongst other things, offers a quote from Henry James's *Transatlantic Sketches* in which James reports on his experience of the Netherlands: 'All these elements of the general spectacle in this entertaining country at least give one's regular habits of thought the stimulus of a little confusion and make one feel that one is dealing with an original genius'. For Soja, who lived for a while in Amsterdam, Dutch culture represents – visibly in its historic topography – what he calls 'an insistent tolerance'. Soja offers as a kind of emblem of Dutch culture the Beguine Court, or *Begijnhof* – a quadrangle of alms-houses enclosing a flower-filled garden with central lawn, and including two churches. One dates from the fourteenth century, is the site of a miracle in 1345, and was rebuilt at the beginning of the seventeenth century. The other is of mid-seventeenth-century origin. This is a place of both orderly transgression and transition. The first church was where the fleeing English Pilgrim Fathers prayed before setting sail on the Mayflower. The second was a refuge for Catholic sisters escaping post-Reformation Calvinist purges. The Court was founded in 1356 for the Beguines, a lay sisterhood who sought a convent-like life but were free to leave and marry if they wished. Soja continues: 'Today, the *Begijnhof* continues to be home to *ongehuwde dames* (unmarried ladies) who pay a nominal rent to live very comfortably around the lawned quadrangle. Despite the flocking tourists, it remains a remarkably peaceful spot, a reflective urban retreat that succeeds in being both open and closed at the same time, just like so many other paradoxical spaces and places in the refugee filled Amsterdam Centrum'.[35] In other words, the *Begijnhof* signifies an uncanny space which manages, and has managed through seven hundred years, to tolerate the paradox of absolute propriety and scandal, one law and another opposing law, in the same place at the same time. For Soja, the Beguine Court seems to emblematise a space (once again associated with women) which exemplifies the *spirit* of carnival as that might be lived, non-riotously, in the day to day.

In 'The Disorder of Uses; a Case History of Clutter',[36] Adam Phillips opens with a quotation from William Empson's 'A Note on a Commentary on Hart Crane's "Voyages III"': 'I think your analysis is right as far as it goes but if completed leaves no word which is at all meaningless'.[37] Comparing psychoanalysis to the instruction manual, or conduct book, in which the analytic urge consists in a pragmatic clarity, Phillips wonders about psychoanalysis's problematic relation to mess and disorder: 'Psychoanalytic theory – and, indeed, its highly ritualized practice – has an aversion to clutter. Its categories of pathology are always fantasies of disorder (there is, for example, a well-known diagnostic category called a character disorder, as though character could be anything else)'.[38] Psychoanalysis, Phillips says, 'repudiates chaos'. Yet, he continues, the disorder of clutter invites us to do something else, 'something puzzling, or even uncanny; that is, to make meaning – as in, just say something about – the absence of pattern. Clutter, like all the orderly disorders we can describe in language, tantalizes us as readers of it. We can't be sure whom the joke will be on if we say something intelligible or persuasive about it'.[39]

Clutter, in Phillips's argument, is about a disorder which wants to bring about *another* order: 'when we are talking about clutter we should remember that anything that stops something happening is making something else possible, that if you lose something you might find something else in the process of looking for it. Indeed, this may be the only way you can find something else'.[40] This nicely echoes the scientist Alexander Fleming's 'One sometimes finds what one is not looking for'.[41] It seems to me that what Phillips pursues in his essay is a generous and tolerant view of mess and disorder. Disorder is the condition of finding another, different – perhaps radically different – order. It is what Phillips calls a 'technique for the uncalculated'. A little later he says 'A good life, one might say, involves making the messes you need'.

It is with what Phillips, in an essay in his book *The Beast in the Nursery*, calls 'the dreaming self' that we are able to think creatively and purposefully.[42] It is with this self, which, following Winnicott, Phillips sees as one of the best discoveries of psychoanalysis, that we can do a work which is, as it were, non-alienated: 'Dream-work is unforced labour'.[43] It is this sort of work, Phillips implies, which the political economy of modernity has not learned to value sufficiently well. In another chapter from the same book, quoting a letter from the poet John Keats to his friend, Reynolds, Phillips says:

> In this great letter Keats – whose life was trammelled by struggle, but who was keen to be tenacious – is speaking up for, and talking himself into, the virtue of not being conventionally thorough: he is writing as a poet, not as a scholar. His letter is a small manifesto against conscientiousness; in favour of what psychoanalysts might call dream-work and Keats calls, more winningly, diligent indolence.
>
> ... What Keats is at his most leisured pains to say in this letter is how much can be made of what is apparently so little. You don't have to do very much to get things done, as long as you don't need to know what you are doing. If you have too much of a plan you've got a real job on your hands.[44]

Here Keats demonstrates his recognition that work – that is to say productive thought about and in the world – sometimes requires us to go against the rational planning of the ego and the work ethic of the superego; sometimes we can be at our most creative and productive when we are willing to suspend our sublimated drives and allow ourselves to follow what Phillips calls the random and contingent 'hints' which the world offers us. In this way, we can continue with the urgent and constant business of making sense of the world and of ourselves in it, a task which proceeds, as Hegel said, by indirection.[45] Too much rationalisation (too much planning) leaves no room for this sort of essentially human work. A little later, Phillips recounts a conversation between the philosopher Wittgenstein and an American colleague, Bouwsma; speaking of Kierkegaard, whom he describes as 'very serious', Wittgenstein intimates that he finds Kierkegaard's very thoroughness off-putting. On the problem of not being allowed the subtlety of hints, Phillips notes:

> ... when Wittgenstein starts talking about how to do something – in this case ... how to teach ethics – he talks about hinting. The hint facilitates something in him; and he places it in opposition to a certain kind of attention that gives him too much contact with the author he is interested in. He could not read Kierkegaard 'much'; 'He did not want another man's thought all chewed. A word or two was sometimes enough'.[46]

Here, using the insights of psychoanalysis, Phillips offers a certain model of serious work, work of the kind that affects people's understandings of the world – whether through literature or philosophy – which is *not* strictly calculable. In the 1990s, this notion of work is being articulated by businesspeople and economists as well as by psychoanalysts: this is evidenced, for example, in the work of the New Economics Foundation (whose interests lie in social auditing), The Relationships Foundation (who are interested in the profit to be derived from understanding the importance of relationships in business: relational auditing), and the charity Antidote, whose mission commits it to the furthering of emotional literacy. These are all signs of contemporary trends towards a more reflexive form of modernity, as opposed to the continual pursuit of managerialist calculations. In this conception of work, sheer dogged effort might not always be the most effective approach. It is important to be open, as Wittgenstein put it, to hints or suggestions. Koestler is making a similar point in this passage:

> In an old *Alchemist's Rosarium*, whose author I have forgotten, I once saw two pieces of advice for finding the Philosopher's Stone printed side by side:
> – The Stone can only be found when the search lies heavy on the searcher
> – Thou seekest hard and findest not. Seek not and thou wilst find.
> The introspective reports of artists and scientists on their sources of inspiration and methods of work often display the same contradiction ... Souriau's famous 'to invent you must think aside' – '*pour inventer il faut penser à côté*' – quoted with approval by Poincaré, points in the same direction.[47]

Conversely, an economically or managerially dictated conception of work that is aimed at specific ends, demanding detailed plans which are closely time-managed, will preclude the possibility of creative and lifeful solutions to problems; the lack of opportunity for 'idling', 'waiting' or following up 'hints' imposes a sort of deathliness upon both worker and work. It is here, perhaps, that capitalism's contradictions most resistant of solution lie: on the one hand, and as Marx knew, markets responsive to needs and social trends, and innovative in both meeting, anticipating (and creating) what will sell, are tremendously creative. On the other hand, the desire to maximise profits by the planning and focusing of workers' (whether of hand or mind) endeavours leads to a deadening effect upon cultural spontaneity and creativity. The reason for this is that the idea of profit is so limitingly understood by the utilitarian mind-set. J.S. Mill's criticism of Bentham was, precisely, that he lacked *imagination*, and was possessed of the (delusory) 'completeness of limited men'.[48]

In this chapter I have looked at a number of cultural engagements with imagining and mapping the present in ways which uncover the virtues of funny and often feminine places of ordered disorder and creative 'messiness', through learning to resist a mad and over-ordering rationalism (effected in the intrusive overmanagement of the life-world by a 'bad' paternal law). If it is true that, as Adam Phillips says, 'a good life involves making the messes you need', and that this must involve some sense of the logic of a reason which is unconscious or non-calculable, to what extent can we find such a sense emerging in science – the 'truth-language' of modernity? or in a politics which has hitherto believed its policies to be rationally dependent upon scientifically based research? It is to this question of a mourningful politics and a mourningful science that I turn in the two remaining chapters.

In chapter 5, I will look at ways in which business, economics and the relatively new discipline of evolutionary neurobiology are gradually coming to redefine ideas of profit and rationality. There is a growing recognition of the profitability of creative thought; and that, however much ideas must, in the end, be objectively verifiable, their production nonetheless depends, in Koestler's words, 'on mental processes which are subjective, irrational, and verifiable only after the event'. But first I want to turn to the implications of these discussions for the political project associated with the politics of Tony Blair's new Labour.

NOTES

1   See Raymond Williams's charting of these anxieties in *Culture and Society*, Chatto & Windus, London 1958.

2   See P. Sacks, *The English Elegy: Studies in the Genre from Spenser to Yeats*, Johns Hopkins University Press, London 1985, on the increasing difficulty poets encounter in writing mourning poems from the seventeenth century onwards. See also Michel Foucault's references to Baudelaire's perception of modernity as funereal, in Foucault, 'What is

Enlightenment?', in P. Rabinow (ed), *The Foucault Reader*, Penguin, Harmondsworth 1986.

3   C. Baudelaire, 'The Painter of Modern Life' in *The Painter of Modern Life and Other Essays*, J. Mayne (ed & tr.), Phaidon, London 1964.

4   J. Bernstein, *The Fate of Art: Aesthetic Alienation from Kant to Derrida and Adorno*, Polity, Cambridge 1992.

5   S. Freud, 'Mourning and Melancholia', PFL 11: *On Metapsychology*, Penguin, Harmondsworth 1984.

6   See Freud, 'Beyond the Pleasure Principle', *Ibid.*

7   Freud, 'Mourning and Melancholia', 1984, *op. cit.*

8   'New Modernity' is the term used by Albrecht Wellmer; 'second Enlightenment' is a phrase used by Gerald Edelman. See A. Wellmer, *The Persistence of Modernity: Essays on Aesthetics, Ethics, and Postmodernism*, tr. D. Midgely, MIT, Cambridge 1991; G. Edelman, *Bright Air, Brilliant Fire: on the Matter of the Mind*, Penguin, Harmondsworth 1992.

9   Both Jean-Francois Lyotard, in 'Answering the Question: What is Postmodernism?' in Lyotard, *The Postmodern Condition*, (1979), tr. G. Bennington & B. Massumi, Manchester University Press, Manchester 1984, and Zygmunt Bauman, in *Postmodern Ethics*, Blackwell, Oxford 1993, argue that postmodernity (conditions of flux, uncertainty, relativity of values, etc) is the necessary *condition* of modernity which is, itself, the labour of organising meaningful narratives.

10 G. Rose, *Love's Work*, Chatto & Windus, London 1995.

11 A. Light, *Forever England: Feminity, literature and Conservatism between the wars*, Routledge, London 1991.

12 For a more detailed account of Bill Unwin's Freudian paternal identifications, see my 'After Grief? What Kinds of Inhuman Selves?', *New Formations*, 25, (Summer, 1995).

13 P. Sacks, 1985, *op. cit.*, p17.

14 P. Waugh, *Harvest of the Sixties: English Literature and its Background 1960 to 1990*, OUP, Oxford 1995.

15 'In 1970, in a talk [Winnicott] gave to Anglican priests, he was asked how he would tell whether a person needed psychiatric help. "If a person comes and talks to you", he said, "and, listening to him, you feel he is boring you, then he is sick and needs psychiatric treatment. But if he sustains your interest, no matter how grave his distress or conflict, then you can help him all right."' A. Phillips, *Winnicott*, Fontana, London 1988, p25.

16 J. Culler, *Barthes*, Fontana, London 1990, p98.

17 D. W. Winnicott, 'True and False Self', in Winnicott, *The Maturational Processes and the Facilitating Environment*, Karnac Books, London 1990, p147.

18 T. Eagleton, 'Capitalism, Modernism and Postmodernism', *New Left Review*, 152, July/August, 1985.

19 P. Heelas, *The New Age Movement: The Celebration of the Self and the Sacralization of Modernity*, Blackwell, Oxford 1996, p36.

20 *Ibid.*, p62.

21 *Ibid.*, p37.

22 M. Bakhtin, 'Introduction' to *Rabelais and His World*, Indiana University Press, Bloomington 1984.

23 In 'Sorties', Cixous describes what she terms two 'realms' or 'economies': the realm of the proper, and the realm of the gift. In the modern world (although not necessarily in a utopian future), these two realms are gendered. Both concern the rules governing exchange. In the realm of the proper (*propre*), exchange occurs within a closed economy in which values (financial, semantic, gendered, etc.) are 'fixed'. Basically, this is the economy of bourgeois values tied to 'propriety' and 'property'. The realm of the gift, on the other hand, is a realm/economy in which values and exchanges are open-ended and fluid. As noted in chapter 2, Cixous's realm of the gift has some obvious affinities with Winnicott's 'transitional space'.

24 S. Freud, *Jokes and their Relation to the Unconscious*, PFL 6, Penguin, Harmondsworth 1976.

25 D.W.Winnicott, 'The Manic Defence', in Winnicott, *Collected Papers: Through Paediatrics to Psychoanalysis*, Tavistock, London 1958, p131.

26 Phillips, *Winnicott, op. cit.*, p60.

27 Heelas, 1996, *op. cit.*, p47.

28 S. Freud, *Jokes and their Relation to the Unconscious*, PFL 6, Penguin, Harmondsworth 1976, p271.

29 *Ibid.*, p270.

30 *Ibid.*, p147.

31 A. Koestler, *The Act of Creation*, Picador, London 1975, p95.

32 *Ibid.*, p96.

33 *Ibid.*, p147.

34 E. Soja, 'The Stimulus of a Little Confusion', a special lecture sponsored by the city of Amsterdam, and the Centre for Metropolitan Research at the University of Amsterdam, *Centrum voor Grootstedelijk Onderzoek*, Amsterdam 1991, p7.

35 *Ibid.*, p9.

36 A. Phillips, 'The Disorder of Uses; a Case History of Clutter', in S. Dunn, B. Morrison & M. Roberts (eds), *Mind Readings: Writers' Journeys Through Mental States*, Minerva, London 1996.

37 *Ibid.*, p151.

38 *Ibid.*

39 *Ibid.*, p152.

40 *Ibid.*, pp152-3.

41 A. Koestler, *The Act of Creation*, Picador, London 1975, p145.

42 Phillips, *The Beast in the Nursery*, Faber & Faber, London, 1998, p58.

43 *Ibid.*

44 *Ibid.*, p66.

45 G. W. F. Hegel, 'Preface: On Scientific Cognition', *Phenomenology of Spirit*, tr. A.V. Miller, 'Forward', J.N. Findlay, Oxford University Press, Oxford 1977.

46 Phillips, *Beast in the Nursery*, *op. cit.*, p70.

47 Koestler, *Act of Creation*, *op. cit.*, p145.

48 Mill is quoting Carlyle. J.S. Mill, 'On Bentham', J.S. Mill & Jeremy Bentham, *Utilitaranism and Other Essays*, A. Ryan (ed), Penguin, Harmondsworth 1987, p174.

CHAPTER 4

Government – as management, or mourning?

Men were not intended to work with the accuracy of tools, to be precise and perfect in all their actions. If you will have that precision out of them, and make their fingers measure degrees like cog wheels, and their arms strike curves like compasses, you must unhumanize them.

John Ruskin, 'The Nature of Gothic' from *The Stones of Venice*

When Ruskin wrote the above words, he had stonemasons' bodies in mind. But the demand for accuracy and efficiency of work, and the demand for predictable products meeting standard criteria which Ruskin identified with neo-classical stone working, is at the heart of capitalist modernity. Calculation rules in the notion that every good and service must be quantifiable, and rationalisation rules in the organisation of the most efficient means of commodity production. The person in charge of all this is, as Alasdair MacIntyre argued in *After Virtue*, one of the three prototypical 'characters' of modernity: the manager.[1] Why should this be so? Consider the differences between a large premodern quasi-feudal organisation such as a family estate with house, farms, parkland and so on, and a large modern organisation such as a plc. In the former, the owner and estate manager are certainly interested in yield – their lives and family fortunes depend on it – but the relationships and allegiances of which it is comprised are largely face to face and must share common commitments and values. There has to be reciprocity in the common endeavour, even if this reciprocity is unequal and hierarchical. What is shared in such an organisation is the common enterprise of keeping the estate in productive order, and this is achieved by everyone fulfilling their proper role and place in the order of things. And this giving expression to role and place in the order of things is not separate from morality; to behave appropriately *is* to behave morally. The, to us, repugnant words of the hymn 'All Things Bright and Beautiful' – 'The rich man at his table; the poor man at his gate; God made them high and lowly, and orders their estate' – perhaps gives expression to the vestigial (and convenient for nineteenth-century capitalists) remains of such an understanding of the world.

Writing of the eighteenth-century Northern European Enlightenment cultures, in which such an understanding of morality still pertained, but was in the process of change, MacIntyre points out that the idea of morality divorced from religion or social place is a relatively recent one. In the Enlightenment languages of the educated – Latin and Greek – 'there is no word correctly translated by our word moral ... "moralis" like its Greek predecessor *êthikos* ... means "pertaining to character" where a man's character is nothing other than his set disposition to behave systematically in one way rather than another, to lead one particular kind of life'.[2]

In other words, in premodern societies, to live *out* of your place and estate in the order of things was to live without an ethos – to live meaninglessly, as if the world and man's place in it had no meaning. Since such would be to deny the existence of gods or God, to live in such a manner would be to live *immorally*.

MacIntyre's argument is that, in modern societies, the lived morality of the pre-modern world is replaced by what he calls the 'moral fictions' of the modern, and these are encapsulated in the modern 'characters' of the aesthete, the therapist, and the manager. Actual discussions of morality – divorced as they are from the historical context and conditions in which they first arose – are simply abstract and interminable. (The aesthete and the therapist need not detain us here; it is the figure of the manager I wish to focus upon at this point.)

In large modern organisations, the desired performance of individuals is not that they should live out their characteristic and unchanging ethos, but that they should be efficient. The guardian of efficiency is the manager. But, argues MacIntyre, the managerial expertise of improved efficiency of the workforce which the manager claims is, precisely, a *fiction*. This will be an important consideration in the argument about contemporary British politics which follows later in this chapter.

MacIntyre's argument is that, since the decline of Aristotelianism, in which to be moral meant to live out your ethos, moral questions derived from a once complete context have become as fragments: free-floating, pseudo-questions. Our response to our moral ungroundedness has been to erect complex illusions of 'expertise', the most pervasive of which is the 'theatre of illusions' of the manager:

> The claim that the manager makes to effectiveness rests of course on the further claim to possess a stock of knowledge by means of which organizations and social structures can be molded. Such knowledge would have to include a set of factual law-like generalizations which would enable the manager to predict that, if an event or state of affairs of a certain type were to occur or to be brought about, some other event or state of affairs of some specific kind would result. For only such law-like generalizations could yield those particular [causal] explanations and predictions by means of which the manager could mold, influence and control the social environment.[3]

As we know, management 'science' is not at all scientific in this way. Rather like economic 'science', the claim to scientific status (not, itself, foolproof) is belied by experience; neither managers nor economists are, in fact, able to predict with any great degree of accuracy what will be the outcome of any particular events or states of affairs. And, as common sense suggests, this is because both deal with the actions of fairly unpredictable combinations of millions of events – more usually known as human beings and their actions. Economist Paul Ormerod's version of this, in his *The Death of Economics*, is that classical economic theory is wrong, and that economies (like brains/minds in the neuroscientific account) are 'ecological' complex non-linear systems.[4]

A question must arise, then, about the continuing extension of the 'ethos' of managerialism – the Total Quality Management view of things – both as a dominating ethos at work and also, it appears, in government. It is true that treating people as discerning consumers improves services. The problem, though, lies with the impact of such an ethos in terms of work and workers, and its effect on politics. In business, efficiency is tied to 'production' – more likely, these days to be production as a service or 'through-put' – and to profit. More darkly, in Foucauldian vein, we may identify the spread of managerialism with the disciplinary aspect of Enlightenment: more auditing, more surveillance, more knowledge, more power. The intolerance of unmonitored time and increase in repetitious self-regulation induced by perpetual auditing may also be regarded as a new form of mechanisation; the melancholic 'iron cage' of modernity internalised as cyborg superego. But what about politics?

A WILL TO MOURN?

There must be a certain tolerance of disorder in the process of recovery from the traumatic disordering of loss. It is the melancholic who suffers from repetition compulsion, not the mourner. In this chapter I want, really, to ask what a mourningful politics might look like.

In British national life over the past few years, there have been several instances which suggest a widespread common will towards the re-establishing of a coherent social world of community which is the mourner's aim. All ritualistically marked, often with flowers, some of these have been to do with actual deaths: the Hillsborough football stadium tragedy, the Jamie Bulger murder, the massacre of infants at Dunblane, the death of Labour Leader John Smith, and, perhaps most extraordinary of all, the death of Princess Diana. There have been other manifestations of this in the symbolic public rituals of winning or losing. Increasingly football seems to provide the occasion, at a local, national, and international level: both Euro 1996 and the 1998 World Cup produced some extraordinary scenes of communal bonding. France's victory in the latter, with its multi-racial team, seemed to turn an immensely significant corner in that country's history of racial tensions. As a resident of Highbury in North London (and armchair Arsenal supporter), I can testify to the remarkable local support for, and response to, Arsenal's double victory in the F.A. and League Cups of 1998. On the Sunday after the F.A. Cup final, Islington was a sea of honking cars, red and white clothing, and pervasive good will. Tying it all together in genial self-mockery, tabloid chutzpah, and acknowledgement of football's internationally mixed modern nature, the *Mirror*'s headline after France's victory ran: 'Arsenal wins the World Cup'. Also, importantly, to be added to this list, is the extraordinary jubilation of Labour's 1997 election victory in which the rotten and decomposing body of British Conservatism was committed to the purifying flames of the funeral pyre. *Everyone* in Britain will remember the symbolic force of the moment when the jingoistic Michael Portillo lost to the openly gay Stephen Twigg. On that warm spring night, early in the hours of 2 May, when windows were open to the world, many of us recall the 3 a.m. *roar* of satisfaction from the neighbourhood.

On a more serious note, socialism – which should be the politics of communal making-good if anything is – has, in the past, suffered from some problems in regard to its self-understanding in relation to any modern will to mourn. In 1995 I wrote of the symbolic illiteracy involved in the 1978-9 Winter of Discontent in which trade union activity left the dead unburied.[5] This refusal of the importance of last rites was as indicative as anything could be of a party pathologically unable to renew itself. It was not until 1994, with the death of Labour Leader John Smith, that a political will to renewal finally found the real and symbolic focus it needed.

The death of John Smith in April 1994 was uncanny in the extent of the shock it generated. The country was more shocked than anyone might have expected. It was, as it were, shocked at its own shock. But there is, I think, an explanation for the force of the collective unconscious identifications that Smith's death released.

Smith's leadership of the Opposition had been, quite evidently and determinedly, a huge work of reparation in a party riven by divisions – ideological and actual – since the early 1980s, a crisis which sharpened after 1989, when the party was haunted by a massive loss of identity and a consequent failure to come to terms with a profoundly politically changed world. As such, Smith's work as leader began, for the Labour Party, the consoling reparations of a radically altered identity which we associate with the effects of loss and its self-shattering, and also with the work of mourning which must follow from that. It signalled the possibility that the Labour Party might have the will to think itself as mourningfully, elegiacally, transformed, and also the Labour Party's will to take up its responsibility of offering an alternative to the deadly havoc that free market conservatism was wreaking upon the British economy and upon the fabric of individual and collective life.

Smith's death shot this mourning-work into a remarkable collective focus, so that it was able to symbolise – in this extraordinary constellation of events – precisely what people had collectively been struggling to articulate in the melancholic nostalgias of the 1980s and early 1990s. Smith's repair of the Labour Party offered, first, a glimpse of healthy mourning, and then, with his death, gave the process symbolic actuality.

It is, thus, unsurprising that Smith's sudden death had the uncanny effect it did, since it gave specific form to a longer history of grief in which he, himself, had become first a benevolent political actor and, secondly, and with stunning symbolic coherence, a decent man who had died too soon. It is equally unsurprising that public life across the political spectrum found itself compelled (with all the force of unconscious motivations) to extensive expressions of grief, and that Smith's burial on Iona – the remote burying place of ancient Scottish kings –

took on mythic resonances. In the sense that myth gives symbolic expression to experiences which cannot be articulated with their full affective force in other ways, Smith's death was mythic. The extraordinary, Chaucerian, talk of pilgrimages to Iona the following April was absolutely of a piece with the symbolic meanings released.

The emergence of Tony Blair as Labour leader in 1994 seemed to signal a commitment to continuing the work of mourning, and Blair's early speeches, with their talk of renewal, seemed to catch the national mood well. The force of reconciliation with which both the Minister for Northern Ireland, Mo Mowlam, and the Prime Minister approached the agreement to hold a referendum on a new government for the province, the outcome of which was the symbolically (Easter as a time of death and rebirth) as well as politically very important Good Friday Accord of 1998, was palpable and impressive.

How, then, is the Labour government which came to power in the early hours of 2 May 1997, and especially its powerful leader Tony Blair, to be understood? In the month leading up to, and including, the first anniversary of the 1997 General Election, five of what Adam Phillips might call 'hints' appeared in the national press in Britain: two of these were cartoons from the *Guardian* cartoonist Steve Bell, the rest articles. The first of the Bell cartoons, produced just after the successful culmination to the Good Friday peace talks in Northern Ireland, depicted Blair walking on water; the second, appearing after the breaking of the story about Gitta Sereney's book on the child killer Mary Bell, and Blair's subsequent condemnation of Sereney's payment to Bell as 'repugnant', depicted Blair as Oliver Cromwell, Lord Protector, Bible in hand. The three articles were a *Guardian* 'Face to Faith' column, 'Why ministers can't manage' by Malcolm Brown of the William Temple Foundation;[6] John Gray's *New Statesman* review of Jack Beatty's book on Peter Drucker, originator of management theory;[7] and an article by Roy Hattersley in The *Observer* 'Tony Blair finally gets some real opposition', based on an interview with the Prime Minister.

Brown's article continued the theme of an article published a few months earlier by Madeleine Bunting, the *Guardian*'s Religious Affairs editor, entitled 'Christians not commodities' (*Guardian*, 25.10.97). In this earlier article Bunting reported the response of the Bishop of London to being asked what was the greatest threat facing the Anglican Church in the 1990s. The Bishop's reply was, unexpectedly, 'the commodification of God'. The Reverend Brown's article begins with a condemnation of the Church's confusion about what modernity means. In it he suggests that, 'The Church of England's current obsession with managerialism only confirms its spiral of decline', and continues by arguing (in tune with MacIntyre) that, as a response to the crises of modernity, managerialism is an irrelevance. Brown also points out the paradox that the 'liberal' impetus for modernisation as managerialism came from the very wing of the Church – the fundamentalist evangelicals – which has been most concerned to 'put the boot in with such zest' to the Church's humane 'liberals'. Here, at the heart of the domain which should be *most* resistant to modernity's cult of managerial efficiency and the false ethos of utilitarian profitability, we find urged the idea that Christian *faith* can be treated as an *efficient commodity* in the market-place of faiths. And perhaps we shouldn't be too surprised to see the fundamentalists' divorce of economic liberalism from socially progressive liberalism since this was precisely the neo-liberalism which Thatcherism introduced. Of course, Brown's 'paradox' is ironic. The philistinism of 'marketing God' presumably arouses in Brown the kind of dismay aroused 140 years ago in Matthew Arnold when contemplating the rise of a culturally narrow capitalist class. Is the hidden hand of God shortly to merge with the hidden hand of the market in the Church of England?

With reference to Alasdair MacIntyre's book *After Virtue* which I discussed earlier, Brown points out that, along with the aesthete and the therapist, the manager is one of the three 'characters' who typify the empty nature of liberal modernity; of all three he says: 'What they have in common is the focus on means rather than ends and the neglect of anything identifiable as an ultimate value, or an ultimate truth'. I would take issue with MacIntyre's *tout court* condemnation of the therapist – not every form of therapy is directed towards self-management alone – but that doesn't alter the central point made both by MacIntyre and Brown, that these approaches to individual dilemmas seek to extract them from the wider understandings and dilemmas of a community and an age. As Brown argues, the cults of the managed self (therapy and aestheticism) or selves (managerialism) lead to the erosion of a *shared* moral language which, instead, is replaced by a (fictional) language of pragmatic 'management'. Thus, in the face of life's dilemmas, the modern managed self makes pragmatic – rather than moral – choices. The criteria for such responses are quite different: moral choice is dictated by what is *right*, by what enables one to live an authentic life, or the good life; managerial choice is dictated by what is efficacious, by what enables one to live an effective or effecting or efficient life – normally in terms of material profit or ease – since the idea of ethical efficiency must strike us as either oxymoron or irony. It is worth noting that one of the effects of the managerialist politics initiated by Thatcherism was to make those occupations which had remained largely vocational, in the sense of being inspired by an ethos, such as teaching or nursing, less and less rewarding. Where the vocation is made subject to managerialism, its passionate human commitments are stifled and drained. The advent of managerialism in the Church implies the end of holy vocation – as Malcolm Brown realises.

But, of course this is not all. As Brown goes on to say, managers 'facilitate the journey'; they do not identify the destination. Where the journey consists of unpredictable and spontaneous interactions between human beings, and when it is precisely these incalculable interactions which will discover shared destinations, as in social relations, management is not simply irrelevant, it is positively damaging. Social relations can be loosely facilitated in any number of ways (good housing, full employment, for example), but they cannot be managed. As Brown points out, study upon study has indicated that markets require a degree of social agreement and cohesion in order to work, but *all* human relations, wherever they occur, exceed in complexity and unpredictability any possible claims to expertise which managers make, and it is in the sphere of free relations that this fact is most obvious.

The language of management is spurious on a number of counts, but, when applied to non-market relations, it is frankly dangerous. In chapter 2 I argued that the practice of comprehensive 'child management' (the totally administered life-world at the heart of Judge Schreber's family) produced 'monstrosities'. It seems quite possible – indeed, it is at the centre of this book's arguments – that the attempt to invade every space of subtlety, creativity, complexity and sacredness, every space where new things are found and made (call it sacred, transitional, mourningful or what you will), may make affectively dead monstrosities of us all. In Malcolm Brown's imagination, as in the imaginations of others, the sacred spark is kept alive by a small group of 'dissidents':

> One is forced to conclude that the evangelical management geeks are the real liberals now. They have adopted and internalised the whole minds[et?] of modernity. Within that mental framework, there are no alternatives; as MacIntyre says, when ends and means have been

decoupled, the capacity to understand and articulate the nature of our situation is lost.

In a managerial Church, authentic faith will be the treasure of the dissidents – the groups that question the foundations of modernity and look to new ways of sustaining the virtues and values of Christian life in a wide-ranging dialogue. Meanwhile, the managers will get on with creating a church conforming to the requirements of global capitalism – and constitutionally incapable of questioning it.

John Gray's 'hint', his review of the book on Peter Drucker, reiterates Brown's points. Drucker (whose work stems from the late 1940s and early 1950s) was prescient concerning the effects of a managerialism which is tied to utilitarian precepts. For example, in 1966, he warned of the risk of managers becoming 'contemptuous of information and stimulus that cannot be reduced to computer logic and computer language'. Gray too cites MacIntyre's anxiety about modern managerialist techniques, that they hopelessly replace earlier moral discourses and consensuses with a mechanical, non-human, view of life:

When society is no longer held together by shared beliefs about the good life, the dominant mode of reasoning becomes instrumental, not moral. Authority comes to justify itself not in ethical terms but simply by its efficacy in achieving stated goals. The prestige of management derives from its claim to possess a kind of general expertise about efficacy. Management studies promises a technology, even a science, of successful action at a time when success has replaced ethics as the test of conduct. For MacIntyre it is self-evident that all such promises are necessarily spurious.

As Gray says, the world described by Drucker's management theory is a world in which effectiveness replaces rightness. But how does all this relate to the world of New Labour and Tony Blair?

Roy Hattersley's 1 May 1998 anniversary article – based on an interview with Blair – unwittingly draws these themes together when he describes Blair as 'not at heart a politician', and, a little later, as acting from the 'conventional pieties of a fashionable clergyman' (i.e. precisely the sort of clergyman whom Brown was criticising above). Hattersley's argument is that 'Blair believes that politics – as traditionally understood and practised – is dead'. The implication in the article is that Blair is driven by something like a *religious* commitment to make the world a better place, but that – rather like Malcolm Brown's evangelical new liberals – he has wholly embraced the managerialist techniques of modernity in order to achieve it. But, of course, and as Brown argues, religious ends – belief in the value of each human being simply *as* human, faith in the subtlety and complexity of life and in a God who moves in mysterious ways – is wholly incompatible with the managerial ethos of efficiency. In order to achieve the latter, individuality cannot be allowed to count for much; sometimes, or even often, efficiency will dictate that people must be incited to work more than is compatible with health or happy home life, or, indeed, may be made redundant. For the manager, human beings are too often reduced to functions.

Britons were made familiar with such ideas during eighteen years of Conservative government under MargaretThatcher and, after 1992, John Major. But now it seems that the new Labour government's aim under Tony Blair is not to question the values of modernity and capitalism, but simply to *manage them better*. Hattersley argues that Tony Blair is a decent man who believes that politics and ideology are 'dead', and that the country is in need of a rebirth from its 'old' ideas. Whether consciously or not, Blair seeks to offer the country a kind of secular, efficient clerisy; the same power and single-minded commitment that helped to reform and make the Labour Party electable is now to attempt a similar 'make-over' for the country. But does this amount to any more than a consolidation of Thatcherism?

The implication of all these hints is that the country continues to suffer from the vice of modern managerialism, and that Tony Blair's vision of his role in the political life of the nation is something like that of the new liberal evangelicals in the Church. The Church, rather than resisting the profane solutions of secular life, increasingly commits itself to an ethos of managerialism and commodification in pursuit of economic survival ('let's get bums on pews') at the expense of the spiritual dimension of its work. Politics, on the other hand, begins to look increasingly like an evangelical modern religion – driven by a commitment to 'modernising' its 'Church' by managing it like a product, complete with simplified and heartfelt exhortations to have faith ('Look – trust me'). Curiously, Blair's own religious affiliations (about which, I think, there is no reason to be sceptical) lie in the other direction – towards Roman Catholicism – and it is said that his thinking on social policy is quietly influenced by Catholic social teaching. Having, perhaps, a deeper grasp of critiques of modernity, Pope Jean Paul II has resolutely resisted the liberalising impulse. Could it be that, with the modernisation of the Labour Party apparently successfully accomplished, Blair believes that modernisation works, and is simply unfamiliar with arguments which focus, as MacIntyre's does, on the ways in which its processes inevitably effect gradual moral and social fragmentation? Blair's Third Way (itself a term with religious connotations) looks like an attempt to banish conflict, or at least to hide it. At a lecture he gave on Blair and Isaiah Berlin in December 1998, Michael Ignatieff likened the Third Way to a blanket thrown over the necessary conflicts of politics, which inevitably produces managerialism.

So what is really going on behind the stage management made so easy by the lack of effective opposition after the near collapse of the Conservative Party in 1997? The Northern Ireland Peace Accord and reform of the House of Lords are big and important issues; but what about the really big things, the things which imperceptibly produce changes which so grip us as to alter our very self-understandings? These things are not played out in big ways; they are produced inadvertently; they are what was left out of the account because accountants and managers are not required to see these kinds of goods; they are modernity's aberrant products. When we look at the anxieties expressed about managerialism in both politics and the Church, what we can see through them are anxieties about confusions of purpose. The apparent triumph of capital, especially after the collapse of the Berlin Wall in 1989 and the embrace of capitalism by the states of the Far East during the 1990s, seems to have had the effect of making everyone believe that the only way of being effective lies in imitating the marketing and managerial procedures employed by capitalist institutions. It is as if we are so well trained to be consumers that it is only *as* consumers that we can – to use Louis Althusser's term – be 'hailed'. But the marketing of commodities is always, in the end, the marketing of pleasure and ease, and both politics and faith will always be, in some important sense, about difficulty and conflict. Democratic politics is about the virtue of agonistics – creative argument – as a way of producing political clarity; faith is about being tested.

The inner logic of capitalism is to make everything a commodity, and to sell these as something which will make your life (and especially the difficult parts of it) easy. But how much this essentially narrowed reductive managerialism and marketing leaves out. John Gray, amongst others, has consistently argued that the unconstrained markets which, since the collapse of the USSR in 1989, have been truly global, pursue an ethos of profit which depends upon manage-rialist techniques of efficiency involving redundancy, restructuring, short-term contracts – and gross insecurity. One of the first effects of this is that the institution of the career is fast becoming what Gray calls a 'relic' of bourgeois culture. More than that, in Gray's view, bourgeois culture itself is passing away, and with it the matrix which has supported the development of liberal institutions; as he says: 'I know of no country in which liberal institutions have renewed them-selves over several generations where the underlying society has not been predominantly bourgeois'.[9] History, it seems, has proved Marx both right and wrong: right about commodification and capital's undermining of bourgeois society; wrong that this would lead to revolution, then a utopia. Certainly, the corrosive effect of market forces or social relations, which Marx described in his analysis of the *laissez faire* capitalism of the first half of the nineteenth century, still holds true today, at the end of the twentieth century. As Gray puts it:

> Conservative parties seek to promote free markets, while at the same time defending 'traditional values'. It is hard to think of a more quixotic enterprise. Free markets are the most potent solvent of tradi-tion at work in the world today. As they continuously revolutionize production, they throw all social relationships into flux. Conservatives glorify the incessant change demanded by free markets and at the same time believe that nothing -in family life or the incidence of crime, for example – will be changed by it.[10]

He goes on to remind his readers of Joseph Schumpeter's 'parallel' argument – first made in a lecture given in 1948 – that the develop-ment of capitalism might be incompatible with the existence of what he called an 'intact civilization'.

Unrestrained global capitalism is highly unstable. As Peter Marris argues, *laissez faire* capitalism induces chronic uncertainty.[11] Institutions manage this uncertainty by 'off-loading' it, in the ways described above, on to employees, who, in turn, 'off-load' it some-where in their personal lives – as aggressive consumers, as angry spouses or anxious parents, or, indeed, as wayward employees committing collective or individual acts of industrial sabotage. For Marris, as for all the contributors to *The Politics of Attachment*, all human beings have need of securely attached relationships of one sort or another; we demonstrate this by the importance which we attach to love and stability in our relationships with our children. And yet, perplexingly, and as Marris says, the kinds of relationships which we value socially are, apparently, to be completely turned around as far as economic relationships are concerned. Where the use of a Darwinian language of competition (between companies, for example) might once have made some sort of sense, now we find this language introduced into the dynamics of the firm itself:

> The successful management of the economy depends increasingly on lack of commitment, constant change and instability. These are the qualities that are believed to create a competitive economy. In the US this strategy is often described admiringly as 'lean and mean'. The goal for the successful firm is to make the fewest possible commitments to its workers: that's the 'meanness' part. The 'lean' part is to shrink the size of its core to the smallest number of relationships.[12]

Even on the basis of the Darwinian language invoked, this is a kind of individualistic madness in which competition within the group is raised above the importance of group solidarity. It is rather like advocating the idea that, even in a condition of war, soldiers on the same side should still try to kill each other in the interests of creating a fitter army.

'Lean and mean' is the language of the fighting machine (and also the language of some contemporary proponents of evolutionary genetics, such as Richard Dawkins – see chapter 5) which pursues an idea of the individual based on the individual soldier or the army; but here the metaphor implies something pathological. In the course of becoming a competitive outfit, the company introduces a sickness into its own body, and the economy introduces a sickness into the society which supports it.

In the face of analyses such as these, Blair's notion of modernity as more efficient and creative management of the nation's resources is either laughably simplistic or simply tragic. But, more than this, and if Blair's early undergraduate commitment to the philosophy of John Macmurray still holds good, it is odd. Macmurray's philosophy is built around the contention that to view rationality as an objective and detached mode of thought, somehow separate from and untainted by emotion, is misconceived. He takes issue with the notion that emotion and reason are distinct, even conflicting, aspects of our life. The impulse to keep them separate comes, he suggests, from the fear that, if we do not we risk slipping back into a way of thinking from which we had begun to emerge:

> of thinking that emotions belong to the animal nature in us, and reason to the divine; that our emotions are unruly and fleshly, the source of evil and disaster, while reason belongs to the divine essence of thinking mind which raises us above the level of the brutes into communion with the eternal.[13]

In other words, there is a tendency to associate reason with progress, civilisation and divinity, while emotion is consigned to the realm of what is childlike, primitive, even 'evil'. With some degree of prescience, given that he was writing in the 1930s, Macmurray suggests that, on the contrary, twentieth century human beings have reached a point of development at which we need to understand that our emotional life provides the underpinning for our rational life:

> Thought has begun to doubt its own monopoly of reason. As soon as that doubt enters the very basis of our civilization begins to shake, and there arises, first dimly in the depths of us, but soon penetrating more and more clearly into consciousness, the cry for a new heaven and a new earth. The doubt and the question mark the opening of a new phase in human development.[14]

Could the doubt (Macmurray was writing in 1935) have arisen from the consciousness of fascism as the manipulation of emotions which were uneducated, unintelligent, and, at base, medieval or barbaric? Whether Macmurray was thinking of fascism or not, it is certainly the case that the romantic impulse which arose in reaction against utilitarianism's rationalising 'disenchantment' of the world was also the source of totalitarian 'solutions' in the twentieth century. But Macmurray's point about the importance of emotion – a point perhaps clarified in the neuroscientific research which I will discuss in the next chapter – is not that reason and emotion are opposed, and that too great a valuation of the former is bad, but that to reason well is always to be aware of, and to be sensitive to, the role of feelings. In other words, the objection is not to reason itself, but to a rationality which tries to deny affect *within itself*. Nor does Macmurray aim to elevate the irrational above the rational (there was, after all, an influential argument made by the neo-conservative George Gilder, in the early 1980s, that contemporary capitalism is 'good' (has a 'theology' and, thus, an ethics) because like art and the sacred it is based upon irrational play.[15]) Critics may object that the reasoner lifts himself above the merely personal and affective when he thinks 'from the point of view of infinity', or 'objectively'; the counter-argument is that no human body is disinterested in this way, and that this is a *good* thing because thinking *beyond* the human-ness of our embodied selves – as purely rational and disinterested – is to think a, sometimes dangerous, fiction. The point, in other words, is to think reason and affection as one complex whole, not as absolutely distinct or opposed.

In a letter dated 18 October 1930, to his friend and mentor Richard Roberts, Macmurray wrote that, so far, we have only liberated thought, and that as regards our understanding of emotional life we remain premodern. We have, he said, developed a science of vast power; but because our understanding of our affective lives is so limited, the uses to which we put this power 'are mostly perverted, or stunted, or vulgarised':

> It is the emotional life of our world that is the danger spot: and it is freedom that it needs if it is to grow and grow straight. I mean that we must stop dictating to people the way in which they come to feel, and instead we must insist on expressing, in speech and action, the feelings that are really in us.[16]

Today, more than sixty years on, there is a decided growth of interest in Macmurrayish ideas and a much wider acceptance of the importance of emotional literacy. For example, in his review of *The Kennedy Tapes: Inside the White House during the Cuban Missile Crisis*, Thomas Powers notices that, *in extremis*, people do not actually proceed in a *simply* or *obviously* 'rational' manner.[17] Even if we take the most sceptical view of self-interest, and assume that these people do not feel history and the future of millions upon their shoulders, here are men whose own lives, and whose families' lives, are *really* at stake. Their task – let us be clear – is to avoid the possibility of World War Three; yet what Powers discovers in the tapes is an extraordinary seriousness accorded to a process which can only be described as intuitive. In a *very* serious situation, reasoning is not explicit but appears as the exchange of 'emotional semaphore', Describing instances of this, Powers says:

This exchange is elusive; its exact meaning seems to hover just out of reach. Other passages are simply incomprehensible as Kennedy's advisers converse with each other in a semi-coherent shorthand of sentence fragments, truncated questions, vague allusions, swallowed words, repetitions, deferential nods and shrugs and miscellaneous noises of objection, assent, qualification, emphasis. There are pages so opaque and unrecoverable that it seems one could evolve a whole new perspective on spoken language as depending less on grammar and syntax than on a kind of emotional semaphore.

What becomes clear in the course of these often tedious discussions is that men in groups don't so much try to figure things out – an intellectual process depending heavily on articulation – as feel things out: to weigh what they are planning to do, and their reasons for doing it, by consulting their gut.

In the next chapter, I argue that 'consulting your gut' is actually a fundamental part of reasoning – and not in any metaphorical sense: work on the role of peptides in the body and brain, undertaken by Candace Pert and colleagues at the National Institute of Mental Health at Maryland, suggests the need for a far-reaching revision of the ways in which we think about the old distinction between feeling and reasoning.[18]

Geoff Mulgan, since May 1997 installed in the Policy Unit at Number 10, has – in his 1997 book *Connexity* – made an extended version of the argument offered here. 'Soft' knowledges, emotional literacy, and all the forms of human relationship skills which are, strictly speaking, incalculable, are increasingly important in contemporary societies. In a chapter entitled 'Ecologies of Mind', Mulgan concludes by saying:

> In a modern liberal society we see ecologies of mind as somehow outside the realm of politics and of conscious choice. The choosing individual is sovereign. But in densely populated societies, this is not a sustainable perspective. We depend on the minds of others, on their being healthy and well-intentioned. The implication of taking these ecologies seriously is that every institution is open to judgements: it becomes legitimate to ask what mentalities they tend to create, whether they leave those who come into contact with them stronger or weaker, more able to bear responsibilities or less so, ethically fluent or ethically stunted. If they drain, suppress, destroy the human spirit then it is

legitimate to ask them to make up the cost they impose on everyone else.[19]

For Mulgan, such ecological 'mentalities' (understood in the broadest sense) constitute 'social capital'; but the term may be misleading since such 'social capital' cannot, in fact, be bought – only acquired through time and affection. Significantly, Mulgan himself turns to the parent-child relation as the model of good or bad 'mentalities': 'The starting-point for understanding mentalities is childhood. It is at an early age that we learn to make connections with others.'[20]

How this relates in practice to the New Labour doctrine of efficiency is another question.

KNOWLEDGE AS IGNORANCE

There is a Robert Heinlein short story in which some scientists discover a way of bringing someone back from the future, for fifteen minutes. They successfully retrieve a scientist from the middle of the third millennium, and begin to question him: 'Have you sorted out the energy problem?' they ask. 'Why, yes', he replies, 'We get energy absolutely free.' '*How did you do it?*' the twentieth-century scientists ask. 'I don't know' replies the scientist from the future. 'Well, what about cancer?' they ask. 'Did you discover a cure for cancer?'. 'Oh yes,' replies the scientist, 'but I'm afraid I couldn't tell you what it is'. The twentieth century scientists try a few other pressing questions in their fifteen minutes – all to no avail. Eventually, after about ten minutes of fruitless questioning, the scientist from the future says 'Look, I'm a heated food scientist. Would you like me to tell you about that?'

Earlier in this century, Max Weber offered another version of this story. In order to understand it, it is necessary to know – as Gray on Drucker points out – that the manager models himself upon the scientist; faced with necessity of understanding and rationalising an organisation, the manager (at least until very recently) analyses, compartmentalises, and breaks it down into units of function. S/he intellectualises, rationally – that is to say without addressing incalculable *human* things – how the institution, organisation or corporation, which s/he is called upon to manage, works. But this scientific model, inasmuch as it is not able to take account of larger and wider human considerations, is flawed. The *nature* of the manager's knowledge – like everyone else's – is *limited* because the instrumentalism of his/her function prevents him/her from addressing wider concerns. Not only does the manager not know enough about how things connect in the wider sphere, s/he is explicitly enjoined to be limited to immediate, let us say short-term, effectiveness. As Weber puts it, the increasing complexity of the modern world means that each individual knows *less*, not more, about the workings of everyday life. No-one, least of all managers who have no specialised knowledge beyond that of managing specialist functions which they, themselves, do not understand, really *knows* how the world *works*. As Weber argues, the 'savage' knows 'incomparably more' about his world, and about how to gain sustenance from it, than any 'modern' knows:

> The increasing intellectualization and rationalization do *not*, therefore, indicate an increased and general knowledge of the conditions under which one lives. It means something else, namely, the knowledge or belief that if one but wished one *could* learn it at any time. Hence, it means that principally there are no mysterious incalculable forces that come into play, but rather that one can, in principle, master all things by calculation. This means that the world is disenchanted. One need no longer have recourse to magical means in order to master or implore the spirits, as did the savage, for whom such mysterious powers existed. Technical means and calculation perform the service. This above all is what intellectualization means.[21]

In highly complex societies, where nobody has the will or knowledge to grasp the larger picture, the impulse to *manage* in a limited way is understandable. But Blair's managerialism is more complex than simply that of the person obliged, by his function, to do what he must.[22]

Blair's managerialism is that of someone imbued with a sense of corporate mission. In this it is similar – as commentators have noted – to Margaret Thatcher's quite evident sense of destiny. In line with the analysis offered so far it could be said that Tony Blair is like a man with a calling – a vocation; but, despite his own Christian commitments, he seems to lack the larger world view or faith which a man with a vocation should have. To have a vocation to manage seems like a contradiction in terms. As I have argued, the manager by definition can have no large view; his/her vision is restricted to the success and efficiency of what s/he manages – whether corporation or country.

THE THIRD WAY: FACILITATING THE JOURNEY WITHOUT IDENTIFYING THE DESTINATION

Earlier in this chapter I referred to MacIntyre's understanding of the manager's task as 'facilitating the journey without identifying the destination'. Early in 1998, Downing Street asked Nexus – a network of left intellectuals, mainly academics – to organise an e-mail debate on the idea of The Third Way. The provenance of the term is varied, but it seems that Blair introduced it into a speech following upon US President Clinton's use of it. Participants in the debate were invited to discuss, or rather to attempt to flesh out, what the term might encompass. Some of those involved in this discussion thought that this might be an invitation to encourage intellectuals to put flesh on something resembling precisely the vision (or ideology) which seems to be so lacking in the new Labour Party. During early May 1998, twenty-six of the participants were invited to Downing Street to present the Prime Minister with the fruits of their deliberations. The *Observer* published an abridged version of one of the papers by journalist Charles Leadbeater – which apparently met with Blair's approval. In an accompanying piece in the paper, Andy McSmith suggested that

> The prime minister is consciously following in the footsteps of Margaret Thatcher, who fought her way to power armed with a determination to win and only a vague idea of what she stood for. Once in office she enlisted intellectual help and hit upon privatisation as the policy which symbolised all she stood for, and invented Thatcherism.
>
> Blair is not vain enough to want to give birth to 'Blairism', but he does want to be seen directing a change in the public mood as fundamental as that which took place in the early 1980s.[23]

Leadbeater's paper suggested that the Third Way 'should not attempt to be a finely calibrated political philosophy, nor should it be a fully engineered ideology. It needs to set out the core beliefs and values which will sustain the Centre-Left's hegemony in Britain and beyond. The central ethic of the Third Way is disarmingly simple: "co-operative self-help"'. Speaking of the promotion of processes of 'creative collaboration', Leadbeater cited the Northern Ireland Peace Talks as an example of Third Way action:

> It only works by being inclusive. Parties to the agreement have rights, but only if they fulfil responsibilities. The settlement promotes self-

governance and devolution of power. The government has helped to set the framework, but the settlement will only work if it is enacted in civil society: state and society must work together. The settlement is not just a political process but a cultural one as well: it will only work if people renegotiate their sense of identity.[24]

This, and the tone of the rest of Leadbeater's paper, exemplified Roy Hattersley's claim that Blair's political mode corresponds to 'an elegant version of pub talk – "why can't they end the squabbling and work together for the good of the country?"' – or 'the conventional pieties of a fashionable clergyman'. People are to be co-operatively creative, and to help themselves by helping each other; public and private sectors shall work together; creative individual shall work with creative individual in recognition of their interdepence; and, presumably, the lion shall lie down with the lamb. It is, unsurprisingly, on the question of the economy that the Third Way has nothing to say. Leadbeater acknowledged this:

> Does the Third Way have a distinctive economics? This is the largest gap. The answer is: no. This is troubling. No political position has long commanded British politics without a distinctive account of how the economy should be organised. The economics of the Third Way must start from the recognition that the most important sources of wealth in the new economy are human and social capital. The British economy is dematerialising before our eyes: its output and assets are overwhelmingly intangible. Services will soon account for close to 80 per cent of the British economy.

But here's the rub: putting flesh upon the idea that the country's most important sources of wealth in the new economy are 'human and social capital' must imply, as I will argue more extensively in chapter 5, a very different idea of what counts as profit. Encouraging creativity in the workplace, or auditing for the quality of a business's impact upon the community and the environment, or auditing the value placed on human relations within an organisation, must mean a substantial change in the manager's task. Under these new criteria, efficiency cannot, any longer, simply mean profit in old-fashioned economic terms (although new age and social and relational audit proponents would say that attending to human and social capital increases economic profits). With these new criteria in view, the manager has to become a different creature: one who attends to human beings as ends rather than as means.

The Third Way debate, in other words, opens up questions of human creativity and well-being which are problematic for a government committed to affirming the unassailability of capitalism. Valuing human beings means valuing human needs for institutions capable of supporting a reasonably secure – material and/or metaphysical – life. By creating intolerable levels of uncertainty and insecurity, the creative but anarchic forces of global capital *weaken* such institutions. The ethos of the commodity leads to a weakening of the possibility of ethical commitments; goods are things which can be bought and sold, and which can become redundant – upon which they will be replaced with newer models: these are not the qualities of a coherently lived life. Indeed, the idea of coherence – sticking together, sticking with something, commitment – becomes an anathema within the ethos of individualism and choice. In an age of choice, commitment – that is to say, affective investment – is redundant.

Investment comes to be understood solely in crude economic terms: one invests as long as there is a tangible material profit. The commodity becomes a fetish which *stands in* for an ethos. As I describe later, one buys a medieval candle-stand and this *stands in* for, as part-object, the ethical life one desires but cannot, under the terms of modernity, live. John Gray writes of the end of the career, and there is much tough talk about the 'portfolio' of jobs which replaces the life-long career; but we know that unemployment, and employment instability, are bad for relationships (inside and outside work), and that the insecurity further strengthens the power of capital and its senior managers at the expense of employees and trade unions. In the face of this, we reach out for the iconic part-objects of a life and world we cannot have.

In an interview with Martin Kettle later in May 1998, the prime minister's response to a question on the Third Way was to say he knew precisely what it was.[25] The Third Way was, apparently, not simply a way between *laissez-faire* and the old Labourist left of 'state control', with everything run through the centre; it was also a third way between two kinds of left 'positions': principled but unrealistic, and pragmatic but perhaps ethically compromised by its slow reformism. According to Blair, the Third Way includes the principles of the 'unrealistic' left – 'social justice, solidarity, community, democracy, liberty' – but 'recast' and 'reshaped' for the 'new world'. The prime minister claimed that the outlines of the Third Way were already evident in policy, but the examples he gave boiled down to a celebration of globalised capital alongside 'prudent' management of the economy, with some added investment in education and training. In other words, global capital has triumphed and the only sensible response from government is to accept that fact and to do what can be done to equip people to be more competitive 'players' in its game. This is government as facilitator, as efficient manager. It does nothing to address the problematic effects of capitalism discussed above.

As Michael Schluter points out, capitalism tends towards 'giantism' and towards the disruption of relational bases on a number of counts – all of which are destructive of human face to face encounters and the securities which spring from these. As Schluter says (and many other economists are increasingly coming to see), traditional economics longs to be scientific and 'Newtonian':

> it would like to have financial systems reduced to a set of coloured buttons with labels like *tax, interest rates, inflation, wages, investment* and so on, and a little booklet that tells the financial mandarins which ones to press in which order to keep the economy on a steady upward path. The reason the economy doesn't behave like this, and why the gurus that governments listen to, like Keynes and Friedman, have ended up with egg on their faces, is of course that the economy isn't a Newtonian system at all: it is Relational.[26]

But if classical economics lacks an understanding of the human element, the new economics advanced by, for example, the New Economic Foundation (NEF), or Michael Shluter of the 'Relationships Foundation', or Paul Ormerod, is far more sympathetic to the more holistic view of the economy as a non-linear system. It is a great pity that the common sense 'pragmatism' with which Tony Blair accepts the continued existence of global capital doesn't extend to an acceptance of the importance of the human beings and environments within which capitalism operates. All of the 'good' left values which Blair sees as being carried over and incorporated in the Third Way are relational values, and at present capitalism is largely uninterested in these. Social justice, solidarity, and community are very obviously relational, but democracy means accountability. Capitalist organisations are accountable only to their shareholders – and this only in an indirect way since shareholders are often institutions themselves. In order for democracy to have a serious meaning in the modern world, capitalist organisations must be accountable in a wider sense, and profit must be calculated in terms broad enough to take account of human lives and social and natural environments. Without this, the prime minister's roll call of left virtues is meaningless.

SOLUTIONS?

What Margaret Thatcher accomplished ideologically was to make certain ideas, or positions, laughable. Thus, for example, in the 1980s the idea that people might be more interested in the commonweal than in their own, improved lives was demonstrated as risible. People wanted to own their own homes; people wanted to be the makers of their own lives. What new Labour needs to do is, similarly, to make certain ideas risible. Amongst these might be the idea that man is an island. As Peter Singer pointed out in the 1998 London School of Economics Darwin Lecture, working with the grain of human nature means acknowledging people's generous social motivations as much as their more self-interested ones. Singer's *How Are We to Live?* also urges the importance of reciprocity (both positive and negative) in the maintenance of co-operative social relations; his favoured principle is the so-called 'tit for tat' rule which, as expressed by Axelrod, is that people should 'enter into all relationships co-operatively, and, thereafter, always respond in the same mode (co-operative or unco-operative) offered by the other person'.[27] However, such behaviour depends upon *accountable* relationships – i.e. relational proximity of one kind or another – and such relations are precisely those which are increasingly attenuated in modern societies of high mobility, large organisations and centralised (more 'efficient') systems. This is economic efficiency in the narrow view, and it leaves out a great many of the things which apparently matter quite a lot to human beings. Indeed, the cultural symptomatology of these needs during the 1990s in Britain is manifested in the widespread commodification of items suggestive of things magical and/or spiritual and/or natural in retail outlets to be found on our high streets and in our shopping centres.

MOONS AND STARS AND OTHER THINGS: KISSING THE WORLD BETTER

Some time in the 1960s, my mother – advocate of that unlikely mix of psychoanalysis and astrology which produced the intense 1960s interest in the work of Carl Jung – took me, excitedly (because here was evidence of a new, popular and marketable, interest in the esoteric ideas which she considered important), to a new bookshop in Camden Town. This bookshop – Compendium – launched upon the market ephemerides (plural of ephemeris – the annual book of tables detailing the movements of the planets, used by astrologers to draw up astrological charts) which had previously only been available via very limited specialist outlets. In the 1960s the shop's entire facade was covered in a sort of hippy, flower-power mural, making it very much a part, together with the open-air market near Camden Lock and the Roundhouse at Chalk Farm, of the celebration of alternative sub-culture and entertainment that was north Camden in the mid to late 1960s. People living alternative life-styles made what they could by selling (gorgeous) second-hand clothes, or home-made hippy candles, or goods brought over from India in the wake of the obligatory guru-pilgrimage of the period. Stars and moons and fairies were everywhere; almost everyone read Tolkien's *Lord of the Rings*.

Compendium bookshop is still there today: astrology and alternative everything at the back; heavy critical theory downstairs. Twenty-five or so years after my first visit, in 1993, I returned to it for some books I needed (downstairs department) and, afterwards, wandering around Camden Town, I realised that the shops (the stalls of Camden Lock market having been translated into bricks and mortar now) were full of stars and moons again. The old hippy candles were back, supplemented this time by candles and candle-stands of a more frankly medieval and ecclesiastical sort, the kind once only available from a church outfitters in Victoria; India was also well represented again, by jewellery, incense, and clothes. The difference was that what we had once thought of as the stuff of an *alternative* culture – alternative to *capitalism*, was now very obviously commodity. What, I asked myself, was going on?

For a brief time, exemplified by the golden summer of 1967 when anyone wearing a kaftan and beads was your *friend*, man, kids like me really believed that we would be able to love the despised world of the adults, of the 'straights' in their suburbs and suits, and of the West with its wars and murderous nuclear hatreds, *better* again. Joni Mitchell sang 'By the time we got to Woodstock, we were half a million strong'; the British contribution to the first global TV link-up was the Beatles, with a studio crammed full of friends, singing 'All You Need is Love'; and, a little later if memory serves, John and Yoko would have bed-ins and bag-ins, and all the other forms of love-ins through which we flower children pursued our liberatory credo.

It is often said these days that the young are depoliticised or that they express their 'politics' in different ways – single-issue campaigns, rebellious celebrations of drug culture, green politics, and so on. But the youth of the 1960s were no different: party politics was for the 'straight'; going on CND marches did not, for most, lead to joining the Labour Party; taking illegal drugs was for personal enlightenment and to put two fingers up to the Establishment; tree-hugging (usually when stoned) affirmed both different ways of experiencing living things, and also an alternative way of valuing life on earth. The predominant impulse of the mid to late 1960s was to search for spiritual and cultural authenticity, for a place that capital couldn't reach.

Wandering through Camden market in 1993, considering all the stars and moons on sale together, with the late addition of kitschy Christian iconography, and the *decorated* utility articles such as calculators with multi-coloured plastic jewels for buttons, it all seemed to me evidence of a desire to retrieve that brief and youthful period of hope when we went about trying to kiss everything and everyone better, of a longing for symbolic enrichment, and a rejection of the dominant utilitarian and neo-economic-liberal culture of the post-1979 period. But the present day-commodification of 1960s hippiedom can only express, via the obscure mechanisms of supply and demand, a hopeless desire *for* that earlier moment and what it signified. That time of optimism cannot be made *real* again; it can only be evoked in object form, then sold; a kind of endlessly unsatisfying political 'retail therapy'.

The problem, as Marx foretold, is that the inexorable logic of capitalism is to commodify or put a price on everything. As became very evident on the night of May 1st/2nd 1997, a great many people believed that something in what Tony Blair said, and what he stood for, might allow us to escape – even if only a little – from the debasing worship of the market, and from its accompanying devaluation and degradation of ethical life. In other words, I believe that, in the 1997 General Election, what was expressed was some form of desire for a way of living in which the good life is not reducible to possessions, greedy getting, or simple self-interest; in which other not *strictly* calculable qualities are seen to have value. For, clearly, it is in the territory of things which cannot be priced that resistance to the ethically enfeebling rule of the cash nexus is to be found. Political commentary, criticism and gossip since the election has really revolved around the question of authenticity and principles. Does the

Blair government have integrity at its core (pictures of Tony and Cherie on their knees at church on Labour Party Conference Sunday 1997), or has Blair simply understood, much more clearly even than Margaret Thatcher, that politics is a commodity like anything else, to be packaged and sold to the punters?

Tony Blair's emphasis on modernisation remains problematic.

THE LEGACY OF THE 1960S AT THE END OF THE TWENTIETH CENTURY – RE-ENCHANTMENT

We have come a long way since the 1960s when the question of human desire and self-expression was first widely raised as a *political* question. Hippiedom sought to resist the most dehumanising aspects of bourgeois commodity culture and the disenchanted world. It didn't succeed, but it *did* popularise a way of thinking about the world which has not only *not* disappeared but which, thirty years later, is being expressed with even greater force – albeit, very often, in commodified forms. Serious and realistic academics and writers (in the humanities *and* in the sciences) have begun the processes of thought, research and publication which feed into what is increasingly a mainstream and level-headed body of work that returns us to the roots of counter-cultural concerns. These roots lie in the perception that what is most valuable about human beings – their creative communicative souls – can never be a commodity upon the market, because the labour of love and relatedness that makes it is *absolutely* incalculable.

What the 1960s set in train on a wide and popular scale was the possibility of thinking human goods differently. What this meant was that enchantment and love were 'in the air', as something resistant to the affective violences of bourgeois life, because uncommodifiable. Capitalism *will* try to commodify the soul – witness the presence in the shops of kitsch Catholic iconography on candles, keyrings, or the clerical managerialism mentioned earlier. This is not because the cash nexus is simply evil – capital is immensely inventive and creative in its own ways – but because, as with Louisa Gradgrind and James Harthouse in Dickens's *Hard Times*, its philosophy turns the heart to ice. The *coup de grâce* of capitalist commodification will lie in obliging it to recognise non-Faustian space – the unpurchaseable place – and thus in obliging it to recognise the unquantifiable – that is *price-less* – value of its absolute 'other': the spaces which *escape* commodification. Here, the logic of commodification would reach its limits, and would reach something like Hegel's attained community of mutual recognition in which the absolute other cannot be mastered, but can only be – *must* be – simply acknowledged *as* absolutely other – and *absolutely* valuable on that account.

Tony Blair has said that people expect too much of governments; yet it is clear – eighteen years of Thatcherism made it obvious, and New Labour's 1997 Election Campaign made it central – that one thing which governments can do is to set a certain tone which then spreads out into all aspects of society at large. Thatcherism elevated individualism and markets above all else; Blair campaigned on anti-corruption and integrity (which is why the November 1997 Formula One tobacco advertising exemption, following upon a million pound donation to the Labour Party by the Formula One Chief Executive Bernie Ecclestone, caused such a furore). The idea that a government could promote the importance of emotional competence, and the importance of the intangible qualities which nurture such competence, is not far-fetched.

Finally: we cannot return to a pre-modern sense of ethos, but it might be possible to shift the terms of our current social contract: to question the fiction of managerial effectiveness and to replace it with ethical requirements, to recognise an *ecological* ethos of interdependency – within and between social and natural worlds – which, as in earlier feudalist modes, recognise the human importance of mutuality, reciprocity, responsibility and obligation, as well as creative individuality and rights.

If we accept the ideas of evolutionary biology, that we are not only selfish but also *social* and co-operative creatures, and try to build on some of these insights within a political context – for instance fostering a sense of mutuality and reciprocity through mechanisms like devolution and proportional representation – we could well manage, to paraphrase Dickens's Sleary, to 'make the best of us, not the worst'. We are not simply the rational beings of neo-classical economics, and for good reason. If we were, we would never be able to work together as the social creatures we have actually evolved into.

If the modern manager – particularly in politics – can be persuaded to recognise the more creative values being explored in contemporary science, and to take *these* scientific knowledges as a model rather than older modern scientific accounts of rationality and rationalisation, it might be possible for the manager's task to involve *different* fictions, and ones that are closer to a human, rather than an inhuman world. It is to some of these developments in the contemporary sciences that I finally turn.

NOTES

1   A. MacIntyre, *After Virtue: A Study in Moral Theory*, Duckworth, London 1981.

2   *Ibid.*, p38.

3   *Ibid.*, p77.

4   P. Ormerod, *The Death of Economics*, Faber & Faber, London 1995.

5   W. Wheeler, 'Dangerous Business: Remembering Freud and a Poetics of Politics', M. Perryman (ed), *The Blair Agenda*, Lawrence & Wishart, London 1996, p115.

6   M. Brown, 'Why ministers can't manage', *Guardian*, 2.5.98, p23.

7   J. Gray, 'After the death of God', *New Statesman*, 3.4.98, p66.

8   R. Hattersley, 'Tony Blair finally gets some real opposition', *Observer*, 3.5.98, p23.

9. J. Gray, 'Hollow triumph: Why Marx still provides a potent critique of the contradictions of late modern capitalism', *Times Literary Supplement*, 8.5.98, p4.

10 *Ibid.*

11 P. Marris, 'The Management of Uncertainty', *The Politics of Attachment: Towards a Secure Society*, S. Kraemer and J. Roberts (eds), Free Association Books, London 1996.

12 *Ibid.*, p193.

13 J. Macmurray, *Reason and Emotion*, Faber & Faber, London 1992 [1935], pp4-5.

14 *Ibid.*, p5.

15 J-J Goux, 'General Economics and Postmodern Capitalism', F. Botting & S. Wilson (eds), *Bataille: A Critical Reader*, Blackwell, Oxford 1998, p200.

16 Macmurray, 1992 [1935], *op. cit.*, ppxiii-xiv.

17 T. Powers, 'And after we've struck Cuba?', *London Review of Books*, vol. 19, no. 22, 13 November 1997.

18 F. Capra, *The Web of Life: A New Synthesis of Mind and Matter*, HarperCollins, London 1996, pp274-7.

19 G. Mulgan, *Connexity: How to Live in a Connected World*, Chatto & Windus, London 1997, p144.

20 *Ibid.*, p132.

21 M. Weber, 'Science as a Vocation', in *From Max Weber: Essays in Sociology*, H.H. Gerth & C. Wright Mills (tr. & eds), Routledge, London 1991, p139.

22 This latter, rather, paints the picture of John Major – who was determined, in every sense, to manage a political situation. Major's calling was, precisely, that of the grey manager, and it ought to be a compelling political story that he failed precisely on that account.

23 A. McSmith, *Observer*, 10.5.98.

24 C. Leadbeater, 'What the wonk told the PM', *Observer*, 10.5.98.

25 M. Kettle, interview with Tony Blair, 'Why we can make a difference', *Guardian*, 15.5.98, p4.

26 M. Schluter & D. Lee, *The R Factor*, Hodder & Stoughton, London 1993, p143.

27 See chapter 7: 'Tit for Tat', in P. Singer, *How Are We to Live?: Ethics in an age of self-interest*, OUP, Oxford 1997.

CHAPTER 5

Rebellious jelly

No wonder that enthusiastic biologists in the nineteenth century, anxious to conclude that there was no qualitative difference between life and chemical processes, tried to believe that the crystal furnished the link, that its growth was actually the same as the growth of a living organism. But excusable though the fancy was, no one, I think, believes anything of the sort today. Protoplasm is a colloid and the colloids are fundamentally different from the crystalline substances. Instead of crystallising they jell, and life in its simplest known form is a shapeless blob of rebellious jelly rather than a crystal eternally obeying the most ancient law.

Joseph Wood Krutch, *The Colloid and the Crystal*

The 'truth language' of modernity has always been science – particularly mathematics and physics. Its favoured techniques have been observation, measurement and calculation, and its favoured model of the universe has been the machine. As I have said before, this has long provoked dissent from people concerned with human imagination and creativity; this, in its very essence, is mysterious and unpredictable, and yet it lies at the heart of what makes us human – symbol makers and users and social beings. Modernity has, then, been notable for the generally hostile relationship between the 'hard' sciences and the Humanities.[1] This has a longish history and is well known. However, and in spite of the so-called cultural history 'science wars' of the 1980s and 1990s which I discuss briefly below, it may be that the rigidities of the 'two cultures' and the kinds of binarism inscribed therein are coming to an end. From the religious naturalism of Spinoza and Leibniz – and particularly the latter's holistic monadology which imagined the world as something akin to an evolving complex non-linear system – to the influence of Darwinism, there has been a thread in the history of modern thought which has promised to lead to what the theologian Don Cupitt describes as the post-Darwinian commitment to 'a non-dualistic view of both the human being and the world'.[2]

Human reason has asserted its ascendancy before, but, as far as we know, no 'modernity' of antiquity ever brought forth the comprehensive loss of a coherent religious world-view in the manner achieved by European Enlightenment since the seventeenth century. In this radical breaking with tradition, the cultures of the West have increasingly experienced a most terrifying loss of spiritual comfort, ethical certainty and social cohesion, and have been more and more obliged to rely, with considerable courage, on the formidable powers of human reason alone. In the contingency of our particular modernity, we might have mourned better than we did; for all that it has yielded, our dualistic and mechanistic modern world-view finds its counterpart in the drained and reduced vision of the depressive. Our frantic desire has been for the melancholic's mastery of an alienated other; and all the differences which humankind has always recognised – of sex, caste, and the varieties of kinship – have fallen easily, in modern times, into melancholia's world of violent and dualistic splittings.[3] In the ancient traditions of elegy, the *successful* mourner is the one who finds 'the ties which bind',[4] and who is able to re-find coherence in a shattered world. What the successful mourner discovers is the possibility of symbolising – that is, making a meaningful language of and for – the world. Perhaps we can say that, although hostilities still prevail, the rash of books popularising science in seductive literary language, and the rash of humanities (mainly American) critiques of scientists as the new priesthood, indicates the early struggle of a new paradigm warring its way into being. It is early days yet, but it seems to me that the counter-intuitive languages of contemporary post-Newtonian physics (whose chaotic Strange Attractors I do not discuss here), and the even more recent languages of contemporary neuroscience (in which language, itself, appears to provide the model of neurological functions), are nothing if not *literary*. And certainly, with the developments in evolutionary neuroscience during the 1990s, it is possible to witness the language of science producing the outline of a coherent non-dualistic account of human being in the world.

It is only out of what is true for modernity that a new truth language and a new modernity can arise. Thus the signs of change which I have discussed so far in this book can only find their grounding in the sorts of truths which are grounded in scientific method. In this chapter, I offer an outline of the present state of affairs in the culture/science *and* science/science wars, and conclude with a discussion of what seems to be the most interesting, fruitful and hopeful area of contemporary evolutionary science: neurobiology. I am not alone in thinking that this research will eventually have far-reaching effects, not only in how we think about ourselves and the world, but also in how we go about our work, leisure and politics. As we come to understand the importance of the ways in which complex non-linear systems such as body, brain and mind develop organically, 'organic' will become one of the touchstones of goodness; not only in relation to food production and consumption where it is already has a strong foothold, but in relation to social developments and group-ings and human relationships of all sorts. As we understand that social health depends upon understanding that *every* living element has effects in a social and natural ecology, we should expect organisa-tions to become interested in the greater creativity of organic relations (facilitated by e-communication) internally and externally; similarly, political activity, organisation and policy development will be concerned with facilitating organic growth; the notion of grass-roots is likely to be radically extended, but not necessarily allied to political parties. Rather, enabled by tropes provided by scientific insights into organic systems development, we are likely to see the development of what Kevin Davey has called 'a networked and poly-centric political agency'.[5]

Of course, it goes without saying that the kinds of thinking which lie behind recent neurobiological research do not only depend upon the recent development of scanners capable of 'watching' the brain-mind in action; they also depend upon the availability of a certain paradigm for looking at the world. In this case, the paradigm is undoubtedly ecology. Both the hard science and the cultural context (that is to say dogged rationality *and* the creative sea of a culture's ideas) are necessary; and it is over the primacy of one or other of these aspects of the making of present and future (neither is primary – they are co-dependent) that the science wars of the late twentieth century have been fought.

In recent years, interest in the sciences – both hostile and friendly – from scholars in the humanities has increased. On the hostile side, in the so-called 'science wars' (predominantly an American affair), cultural studies scholars have been critical of scientific neutrality in relation to ethical questions concerning the applications of scientific research; *and* of scientific truth-claims which are sometimes viewed as simply the hegemonic myths of modern Western culture.[6]

In 1996, in order to expose what he perceived to be a profound ignorance of science amongst cultural studies writers, Alan Sokal, a

New York physicist, submitted a hoax essay to a special 'Science' double-issue of the influential American cultural studies journal *Social Text*.[7] The essay, 'Transgressing the Boundaries: towards a transformative hermeneutics of quantum gravity', was a mish-mash of theoretical jargon, red-herrings and – to the scientifically initiated – plainly senseless. The editors of *Social Text* fell for this Trojan horse and published it, perhaps not so much because they understood it to be a good account of contemporary physics, but because the essay pushed all the right political buttons in a suitably theoretical language, and they so very much wanted to find a *bona fide* scientist 'on the right side'. Sokal himself then publicly declared the piece to be nothing but a nonsensical pastiche of fashionable, postmodern (mostly French) philosophical theory. In early July 1998 the London School of Economics Darwin Seminar invited Sokal to take part in a debate with French sociologist of science Bruno Latour. The result was an absolute refusal to agree on even the most seemingly straight-forward terminology, which seems to be a common feature of meetings between the sciences and the humanities. Perhaps the situation is analogous to what relationship theorists describe as the point of terminal breakdown in a personal relationship, when the partners involved refuse to accept any common semantic referents. At a conference held shortly afterwards at the University of Southampton – 'Darwin's Millennium' – George Levine (a well respected humanities scholar whose work has been centrally concerned with the cultural significance of scientific developments) reported a similar experience when attempting to enter debate with scientists: no sooner was a word out of his mouth than it was subject to radical misunderstanding. In general this was, he said, his experience of such encounters.

And yet, for all this 'two cultures' wrangling, science remains central to our understanding of the world. It is not enough to rail against what is often perceived to be scientific arrogance, and the reduction of human bodies and minds to biological machines. Hard as it is for scientifically untrained critics to penetrate what often seems to be the dry-as-dust world of the scientists, the task remains an important one – not least because scientists are human beings whose pronouncements and ways of interpreting evidence are no less susceptible to cultural influences than anyone else's. This is not meant to indicate an extreme social constructivist point of view, but merely to signal a view – held by some scientists themselves, molecular biologists, microbiologists and neurobiologists in the main – that the relationship between conscious mind and perceived world is more complex than scientific empiricism has traditionally held it to be. Scientific methodology is more rigorous than the impressionistic way of understanding the world employed by most people most of the time, but in the end the scientist's hypotheses and conclusions involve a degree of interpretative activity which is entirely human, and governed by beliefs – that is to say, ways of making sense of the world – belonging to the culture of which they are a part and by which they have been shaped.

Once genetics established the gene as the vehicle of heritability via which Darwin's theory of evolution – random mutation and improved adaptation to environment – could be understood to work, the theory of evolution was firmly established. Politically and socially, Darwinism has been hugely influential. Despite a surprising resistance (even amongst some scientists), we have mostly come to understand that evolution is random and blind – 'any replay of the tape would lead evolution down a path radically different from the road actually taken', as Stephen Jay Gould puts it.[8] For many people, the acknowledgement that human life on earth is contingent has been shocking, as Darwin, for all his attempts to keep it Godly, knew his theory would prove to be – hence his fifteen year delay in publishing. Equally, in the form of Social Darwinism, and in particular in eugenic theory, many people of *all* political persuasions have flirted dangerously with ideas of national and racial purification. More recently, since the publication of E.O. Wilson's *Sociobiology* in 1971, and especially the now notorious chapter 27 which deals with the implications of genetic theory for social theory (and perhaps policy), a particularly reductive and mechanistic interpretation of human evolution has emerged. The sociobiologists, who now call themselves evolutionary psychologists, remain influential.

One of the leading exponents of this icy, bleak, view of life is Richard Dawkins, whose popular *The Selfish Gene* argues that organisms are merely vehicles which have evolved to facilitate their genes' 'will to replicate'. *The Selfish Gene* is a fascinating book which has been a remarkably successful piece of scientific popularising.[9] Its tone is confident and its argument, in the main, is reductive: all plant and animal behaviour is reduced to the single story of evolution as the success of genetic replication. Like almost all 'hard' science, it affects an unelaborated common sense; yet in chapter 11, Dawkins argues that, with the development of culture, humans have made 'replicators' or 'memes' – basically ideas or collections of ideas expressed in word, image or music – which are more powerfully influential even than genes. Genetic inheritance, he argues, is diluted in the common gene pool within three generations, but at the level of culture and ideas, 'The meme-complexes of Socrates, Leonardo, Copernicus and Marconi are still going strong'.[10]

Thus:

> Even if we look on the dark side and assume that individual man is fundamentally selfish, our conscious foresight – our capacity to simulate the future in imagination – could save us from the worst selfish excesses of the blind replicators. We have at least the mental equipment to foster our long-term selfish interests rather than merely our short-term selfish interests. We can see the long-term benefits of participating in a 'conspiracy of doves', and we can sit down together to discuss ways of making the conspiracy work. We have the power to defy the selfish genes of our birth and, if necessary, the selfish memes of our indoctrination. We can even discuss ways of deliberately cultivating and nurturing pure, disinterested altruism – something that has no place in nature, something that has never existed before in the whole history of the world. We are built as gene machines and cultured as meme-machines, but we have the power to turn against our creators. We, alone on earth, can rebel against the tyranny of the selfish replicators.[11]

Dawkins's attachment to the idea of bodies as machines and brains as computers is a direct descendant of the mode of thinking which was dominant in the early Enlightenment of the seventeenth and eighteenth centuries. Although his discussion of memes fruitfully opens out a book which, in its first ten chapters, seemed committed to a rather terrible genetic determinism, Dawkins remains caught within a dualistic view of mind and body in which developing new and better memes is wholly dependent on the rational discussion involved in sitting down in the conspiratorial council of 'doves'. In fact, some of the rational discussion taking place in the field of evolutionary neurobiology (part of the wider development of the science of complexity) challenges both Dawkins's Cartesianism and his idea that the brain is a computer. (Though, indeed, the development of the idea of neural network has altered the ways in which scientists think about computers. More on this subject later.)

Chapter 11 of *The Selfish Gene* (its concluding chapter in the first 1976 edition) reads like Dawkins's (welcome) attempt to become a mourner in a world (that of evolutionary science) that is riven by melancholic splittings. And the field of evolutionary biology also breaks, basically, into two camps: on the one hand the population geneticists, and on the other the palaeobiologists. Niles Eldredge (a palaeobiologist) identifies two opposing camps: 'On one side sit the likes of John Maynard Smith, Richard Dawkins, and George Williams, main exponents of what I call "ultra-Darwinism". Sitting opposite them are people like Stephen Jay Gould, Steven M. Stanley, Elisabeth S. Vrba, and me – all of whom happen to be palaeonto-logists, but belonging to a more eclectic group I have chosen to call the "naturalists"'.[12] Where the geneticists focus on the 'rule' accord-ing to which genetic material is passed on to subsequent generations, and, generally, identify this rule as success in sexual competition, the palaeobiologists' main point of reference is the fossil record which, in fact, is typified by long periods of stability. Given this fact, the latter point to instabilities which 'suddenly' ('suddenly' may be anything from 10,000 to millions of years) occur in complex systems in which adaptation to environment has become more urgent. In this latter view, simple sexual competition in the service of gene replication cannot be a sufficient motor of evolutionary change, since for long periods of time (millions of years) the fossil record indicates no significant change in species. Sexual competition may well be signifi-cant at a 'local' level, but it does not explain large changes in speciation. Probably the most significant contribution to this argu-ment is Stephen J. Gould and Niles Eldredge's 1972 paper on 'punctuated equilibria'. What this paper argued was that evolutionary change leading to the development of new species (of the sort that separates humans from other primates, for example) must depend upon relatively sudden environmental changes and successful (or not) adaptation. Other critics draw upon the concept of 'punctuated equi-libria', and other research findings, in order to argue for a creative dynamism in evolution which involves the interactions of entire bio-spheres. In this view, organisms, environment, and consciousnesses (however limited) *co-evolve* through complex feedback loops. Physicist Fritjof Capra has argued:

> The Gaia theory, as well as the earlier work by Lynn Margulis in microbiology, has exposed the fallacy of the narrow Darwinian concept of adaptation. Throughout the living world evolution cannot be limited to the adaptations of organisms to their environment, because the environment itself is shaped by a network of living systems

capable of adaptation and creativity. So, which adapts to which? Each to the other – they *co-evolve*. As James Lovelock put it, 'So closely coupled is the evolution of living organisms with the evolution of their environment that together they constitute a single evolutionary process.' Thus our focus is shifting from evolution to co-evolution – an ongoing dance that proceeds through a subtle interplay of competition and co-operation, creation and mutual adaptation.[13]

The theologian Don Cupitt has reached a remarkably similar conclusion when he says that, with the historical deferral of a purely objective God in the late Middle Ages (which actually became, for us, the 'late Middle Ages' on precisely that account), and possibly through monkish meditations on the *human* passion of an abandoned Christ on the Cross, a subjective view of the world becomes possible. As others have done, Cupitt argues that in the medieval view of time there can be no vivid sense of history because everything is already fixed as the Divine Plan. People and events are merely actors in an allegory which prefigures the Plan. A sense of history, contingency and the subjective significance of acts can only emerge to the extent that this sense of universal fixity begins to wane. The sources of such a waning are complex, but, certainly, they include – as well as monkish meditations on the personal passion of Christ – the rediscovery of classical philosophies and the rise of Humanism, the Protestant Reformation, the rise of towns as centres of trade and the decline of feudalism, the shift away from martial societies towards the development of civil societies, and – concomitant with all this – the focus upon the importance of manners and constrained personal conduct. With the growth of subjective views of the world, the medieval objective view is, Cupitt argues, deferred:

> The deferral of objectivity, then, allows us to see reality as dialectical. The historical process involves an interplay or conflict of individual projects and world-views, and the so-called real world is the gradually evolving consensus that results. We truly are historical agents, because through our interactions with one another we have among ourselves evolved, and are still shaping, every aspect of the 'reality' within which we live. It is human historical action, rather than divine creation that finishes the world.[14]

These examples, from very different spheres, point to a remarkable synthesis of ideas – the science of complexity – in the making. In the remainder of this chapter I hope to indicate, in a little more detail, ways in which this new 'holistic' approach is taking shape.

EVOLUTIONARY NEUROSCIENCE AND ORGANICISM

I want to turn now to – in my view – the most interesting of all the evolutionists: the neuroscientists who study the evolution of the brain. From the work in this field, it is evident that the evolution of the human brain has depended upon complex adaptive responses to environment which go way beyond any reductive notion of sexual competitiveness. Most importantly, from the evolutionary neuro-biologists' accounts, adaptation and development in humans has involved the development of brains in which feelings derived from experience in the world interact with conscious cognition in complex ways that are irreducible to simple competition. Some of these feelings may be 'basic' – hunger, fear, sexual desire – but the ways in which they are built up, in terms of neural networks consisting of millions of individualised and context-dependent associations, are enormously complex, and thus can account for the fact of human individuality and for the particularly human way of apprehending the world. From this point of view, human creatures and the world in which they live are in a state of constant and developing interaction: the world makes us, and we make and remake the world. As neuro-biologist Gerald Edelman says: 'The objectivist view of the world is at best incomplete and at worst downright wrong. The brain is not a computer and the world is not a piece of computer tape'.[15] And, with echoes of Cupitt: 'The computational or representationalist view is a God's-eye view of nature. It is imposing and it *appears* to permit a lovely-looking map between the mind and nature. Such a map is only lovely, however, as long as one looks away from the issue of how the mind actually reveals itself in human beings with bodies. When applied to the mind *in situ*, this view becomes untenable'.[16] In other words, human beings, or rather their brains, do not receive the world as a fixed pattern of data – which they logically compute to arrive at decisions such as 'good for me', 'not good for me'. Brain-minds *grow* out of bodies which *discover* the world, experiencing infinitely complex feelings which produce infinitely complex psychical associations and defences. Computers do not inhabit sensory bodies and therefore do not learn and grow, as humans do. A computer's binary computational values are programmed in by little gods called computer programmers.[17] In human bodies, 'good for me' and 'not good for me' *become* genetically inherited at a primitive emotional level in the early brain (limbic system), but only because millions of generations of creaturely bodies, with a particular version of 'good' and 'not good for me', survived over time, and long enough to reproduce, on account of a body-learned knowledge about 'good' and 'not good' in the world. In evolution there can be no God's eye, or computer programmer; what is learned, inherited, and *becomes* us, is what is learned on the ground of our being bodies in the world. I shall return to Edelman in more detail later.

A MOURNINGFUL SCIENCE?

The dedication of Adorno's *Minima Moralia: Reflections from Damaged Life* begins: 'The melancholy science from which I make this offering to my friend relates to a region that from time immemorial was regarded as the true field of philosophy, but which, since the latter's conversion into method, has lapsed into intellectual neglect, sententious whimsy and finally oblivion: the teaching of the good life'.[18]

Adorno's regret and anger is directed towards what might be called the 'scientisation' of philosophy: the reduction of philosophy's great aim – of offering an account of the fully human life – to merely either propositional logic or linguistics. Philosophy – understanding the meaning of life – is seemingly still split between science and art, with the former still too often in pursuit of an inhuman (and historically very 'local') computational model of mind, and the latter too often, in the late days of the twentieth century, dumbed down by parody and capital. But perhaps the development of organic complex non-linear systems theories such as those noted by Capra in *The Web of Life* may prove capable of reuniting the different spheres of human knowledge and activity which Enlightenment, in its own moment, found it necessary to put apart.[19]

So are there any reasons for believing that the grim science of evolutionary biology (alongside the 'dismal science' of political economy) might be capable of achieving anything like the mourningful condition – in which reason and affect are reunited in a subtler and richer human understanding of self and world – which I have suggested is a necessary condition of a new modernity? I think there are. There are developments in evolutionary neuroscience which do seem to offer to recast radically our understanding of the relationship between affect and reason, body-mind and world. They offer an approach to science which has, as its central revolutionary understanding, the recognition that truly rational behaviour is *always* thoroughly informed by feelings and 'gut' responses. On its – new – account of mind, the kind of behaviour which proceeds according to a 'rational' theory, while suppressing emotional responses which might rise up in indignation against it, might well be thought of as quite seriously disturbed. But before going on to describe these developments, I want to refer to work in other areas which has helped to provide a wider social and cultural context for them.

COMPLEXITY, HOLISM AND THE 'RATIONAL FOOL'

The closing decades of the twentieth century have seen something like an explosion in books exploring the ending of a Cartesian sensibility, and the development of a more holistic understanding of human beings and forms of organisation. In *Frontiers of Complexity* Peter Coveney and Roger Highfield explain how, 'within science, complexity is a watchword for a thinking about the *collective* behaviour of many basic but interacting units'.[20] In other words, complexity theory tries to understand the movements and developments of any complex systems which are capable of evolving in time. In such systems, the interactions of units lead to 'coherent collective phenomena, so-called emergent properties that can be described only at higher levels than those of the individual units'.[21] Coveney and Highfield point out that in this way we can see that the whole is greater than the sum of the parts. In other words a human being is more than the impulses of his or her genes, and a society is more than an aggregation of individuals. What is clear is that emergent properties are neither entirely random nor disordered (even in the apparently chaotic elements in a system, larger scale orders can be found). As has been shown in computer graphics of very simple nonlinear equations, describing population growths in the context of nearly a million possible combinations of environmental parameters, patterns do emerge. The same holds true in related but subtler chaotic systems: weather, flu epidemics, and the spread of information and ideas are the examples Coveney and Highfield offer. 'Matter', they argue, 'has an innate tendency to self-organise and generate complexity'.[22]

Noting that conventional science, due to the need for ever greater specialisation, tends to be blind to interdisciplinary connections (even within science), Coveney and Highfield point to the development, against these limitations, of a community of scientists – and philosophers – who are 'swimming against this tide' by developing 'integrative thinking',[23] which the authors characterise as 'holistic'.[24]

Mathematic complexity theory, as described by Coveney and Highfield, is still tied to the basic 'grammar' of mathematics. In that language, the complexity of a problem is defined in terms of the number of mathematical operations needed to solve it.[25] The development of complexity theory has, thus, only become possible with the vastly increased calculating power and speed of the most recent generation of computers. Complex systems, as we have seen, are systems which evolve over time and in non-linear ways via complex feedback loops. The most recent work in computational science involves the attempt to programme computers in ways that encourage them to develop their own creative non-linear systems.

It is easy to see how this developing science might have implications for the human sciences, from social policy to business management to economics. For example, because complex non-linear systems have a life of their own in which 'evolutionary success' occurs 'organically' over time, short-term 'rationalist fixes' may cause quite unforeseen disturbances in the wider system. This raises some huge questions for politics and ethics. Unregulated markets, for instance, are clearly based on the Darwinian idea of competition and survival of the fittest; but human societies invoke cultures of value (Dawkins's memes) which transcend ideas of mere brute survival of 'units'. For humans, the survival of certain ideas and practices – which, say, make consciousness of mortality bearable through shared communion or kindness – will be just as important as, or even more important than, any simple notion of the survival of individual 'units' (whether persons or companies). Political interventions in a culture can, thus, never be successful when simply managerial. The manager is directed by the ethos of efficiency as reproduction and survival narrowly conceived, when what is needed for real success is the much broader, and more complicated, vision of human goods which we used to call an ideology. What seems clear is that any new ideology capable of shaping up for the twenty-first century will need to incorporate longer-term views and more holistic thinking. As Coveney and Highfield say:

Comprehending the complexity of life is the biggest challenge facing modern science. What we stand to gain by succeeding in this endeavour is evident. A proper understanding of the living economy of the planet is the key to safeguarding its future. Understanding the living economy of the human body can help to treat it when it is sick. Could a similar understanding of the complexity of human societies aid us in anticipating riots, civil disruptions and wars?[26]

One might also add to their list the task of understanding global economic fluctuations (and what to do about them) better. Unsurprisingly, many economists are themselves coming round to this view.[27]

This emphasis on holism – understanding all life, from the bacteria to the human, in terms of dynamic, creative and interdependent ecologies (Capra's 'web') – is central to what is often described as New Age thinking. It suggests an understanding of the world which goes beyond the melancholic 'splittings' of modernity, one which I would describe – in its attempts at weaving symbolic integrations – as mourningful.

At the level of economics and business practice, perhaps because the focus has shifted away from manufacturing industry to more knowledge-based activities, it is no longer so easy to ignore the human element in economic production. Increasingly, managers and management theorists now devote themselves to thinking about how to build teams and get the best out of people, rather than conducting time and motion studies on the old-fashioned machine model. Paul Heelas describes how, since the early to mid 1980s, there has been a growing interaction between what was once the very strictly scientistic and utilitarian world of business management and the world of self-improvement and quasi-spiritual cults:

> As long ago as 1984, the European Association for Humanistic Psychology, together with the Human Potential Research Project of the Department of Educational Studies of the University of Surrey, ran a large conference on 'Transforming Crisis'. Luminaries such as Peter Russell, 'one of the first people to take human potential workshops into corporations' according to conference material, were involved. The Croydon Business School, to provide a more recent illustration, has run a two week event, in association with the New Age Skyros Institute, on the subject of 'Innovative Management'. (IBM's Tom Jennings was one of the distinguished staff.) And Ronnie Lessem

(1989), of City University Business School (London) has written a volume extolling the principles of 'metaphysical management'. Thinking of my own university, it will be recalled that the Centre for the Study of Management Learning, together with a New Age consultancy (Transform), has run a conference entitled 'Joining Forces: Working with Spirituality in Organizations'. And, in the States, influential author Michael Ray is Professor of Creativity and Marketing at Stanford University. Furthermore an increasing number of articles on New Age management and business are appearing in academic journals. The *Journal of Managerial Psychology*, for example, recently ran a special issue on 'Spirituality in Work Organizations'.[28]

Similarly, at the more theoretical end of the spectrum, economics – once thought of (mistakenly or not) as the epitome of calculative reason – also faces challenges to old orthodoxies from within its ranks. In Britain, for example, the London based New Economics Foundation (NEF) is currently undertaking research on altered indices of well being. And reporting on the Windsor Castle Round Table on Social and Ethical Accounting and Auditing in December 1996, Simon Zadek of NEF wrote: 'Traditional "public relations" is not enough. The public is demanding higher ethical standards from companies. To keep the public's confidence, companies have to prove they are reaching these standards.'

As Heelas's research seems to indicate, the old rationalist notions of what counts as 'profit' and 'loss' are beginning to change. There seems to be a wider shift taking place, moving us from 'individualistic capitalism' to something we could call 'shared profit' capitalism. Under this scenario, the terms 'shared' and 'profit' are likely to be defined much more widely, and both short *and* longer-term goals will begin to figure in the accounting methods of private companies. An example of the new approach can be seen in the development of social auditing, a process whereby an independent body comes into an organisation or company to measure stakeholder – i.e. staff and customers – satisfaction, as well as the impact on the environment and the community, levels of energy consumption, recycling, and so on. Another indication of change is the relational audit pioneered by the economist Michael Schluter, who also set up the Relationships Foundation in Cambridge in 1993, with the aim of strengthening and investing in relationships in a range of key areas, from the criminal justice system and health service to the private sector.[29]

In a similar vein, in July 1998, James Park, director of Antidote, an organisation dedicated to improving public understanding of emotional literacy, addressed a conference on 'The Third Way' organised by the new Labour policy talking-shop Nexus. Viewing the idea of the Third Way as a potential source of new thinking in which policy was not dominated by 'figures' but, rather, by 'qualitative accounts of how people are feeling', Park argued for the significance of a politics of attachment and for the importance of Antidote's project for an 'Emotional and Social Index':

> What we have, at the moment, is bountiful information about economics – how many people are employed, the size of income differentials, what base rates are doing to house prices, etc. We also have some information about the social consequences of the changes taking place in our society and people's ability to cope with them – divorce rates, suicides, levels of depression, absenteeism, crime figures, school exclusions, etc. What we are lacking is the information that would enable us to winkle out whatever connections there may be between these two sets of statistics.[30]

Park argues that we need to examine 'the emotional consequences of economic and other change', 'the social consequences of the emotional consequences', and 'the economic consequences of the social consequences'. His aim is to

> Gather information about what is happening emotionally to a cross-section of individuals in society;
>
> Put that information into quantitative form that will make it possible to look at the correlation with other statistical data;
>
> Enable us to develop hypotheses about the links between these different sorts of information;
>
> Enable us to develop relevant and appropriate systems of support for every group in society.

As Park describes, in this way we could move from a situation where, for the most part, we value only what is measurable, to one where we start to measure what we actually value.

All this, then, should offer some sense of the context – a much more mainstream interest in what Daniel Goleman calls 'emotional intelligence' (in his book of the same name) – within which contemporary neuroscientists are working. Added to this, there is also what Bauman describes as the new 'respect' for the mysterious, the enchanted, and the non-rational, which I have discussed in the second half of Chapter 4.

In addition to this recognition of complexity, and of the need to reconnect reason and emotion, there has been significant work which has helped to bridge developments in economic theory and evolutionary biology. This work also offers a more sympathetic interpretation of Dawkins's project in *The Selfish Gene*. In *The Origins of Virtue*, Matt Ridley notes that, while biologists since the 1960s have moved increasingly towards the 'selfish gene' theory, economists, 'who founded their whole theory on the question "What's in it for the individual?"' have begun to back away: 'Much of the innovation in economics of recent years has been based on the alarming discovery that people are motivated by something other than material self-interest. In other words, just as biology shook off its woolly collectivism [evolution as directed at the survival of the species] and donned the hair shirt of individualism, economics has begun to go the other way: to try to explain why people do things that are against their selfish interests'.[31] Citing economist Robert Frank's *Passions within Reason*, Ridley argues that our emotions have evolved for good reasons: we cannot get by as successful social creatures without a degree of trust, and this often means that seemingly irrational forms of non-calculative human behaviours are important in that they demonstrate commitment to socially important values such as fairness, generosity, and fellow-feeling. Evolutionary biologist Robert Trivers (to whose work Dawkins is also indebted) has arrived at a similar conclusion. As Matt Ridley describes, 'emotions mediate between our inner calculator and our outer behaviour. Emotions elicit reciprocity in our species, and they direct us towards altruism when it might, in the long run pay ... The emotion of guilt, Trivers argued, is used to repair relationships once the guilty person's cheating has been exposed. People are more likely to make altruistic reparative gestures out of guilt when their cheating has become known to others. All in all, the emotions looked to Trivers like the highly polished toolkit of a reciprocating social creature'.[32] In other words, we have moral sentiments because we are social creatures; in Amartya Sen's words, the man of calculating self-interest alone is a 'rational fool'.

These developments and meeting points between neo-Darwinism

and contemporary economics, point to a decisive shift in our under-standing of rationality. There has been a move to reject the limited notion of rational self-interest upon which both neo-classical economics and theories of neo-Darwinian natural selection depend. A narrow focus on rational self interest has led to a situation where, as Robert Frank argues, '[Adam] Smith's carrot and Darwin's stick have by now rendered character development an all but completely forgotten theme in many industrialized countries.'[33]

This resonates with the anxieties I expressed in Chapter 2 about the effects of a violently intrusive hyper-rationalist pedagogy upon 'character development' in the eighteenth, nineteenth and early twen-tieth centuries. In its need to break with the last vestige of the superstitious affectivity of the Middle Ages, the 'first' Enlightenment had a strong in-built suspicion of human emotions. In the long term this seems to have had terrible effects inasmuch as we now have a significant number of individuals ('borderline' personalities) whose affective, emotional lives have been deadened. In the second Enlightenment or new modernity which, I argue in this book, is ahead of us, rational thinking must adapt in order to acknowledge the central significance of feelings in human affairs. But if one of the most important effects of modernity has been to make selves who are in some sense inhuman, this recognition presents us with a huge task. As the next section of this chapter will show, we are now moving towards a much more nuanced sense of what it means to be a human being; but from the errors of the first modernity we have inherited a large number of individuals, and an economic system (unrestricted global capitalism), which have been deformed by that experience. Matt Ridley says that 'A world without obligations to reciprocate, deal fairly, and trust other people would be simply inconceivable'; yet the most unfortunate amongst us will know that a great deal of the modern world is precisely like that.[34] The cultural feedback loops of the modern world's valuation of reason without emotion have, perhaps, made too many monsters or 'rational fools'. In Chapter 4, I argued that the New Labour commitment to 'modernisation' simply fails to understand modernity's *failures*. One of the questions which will, eventually, have to be answered is how political life – that is to say economic and social policy – can make an adequate response to the failures of modernity and modernisation in terms of these new ideas. In other words, how will we deal with our monsters and consign Frankenstein's mad dreams to a yellowed page in a mis-begotten piece of our history? But before we return to the questions of politics in the new modernity, let us turn now to the insights of neurobiology.

THE NEUROSCIENTIFIC REVOLUTION

While evolutionary geneticists such as Richard Dawkins have seemed to promote theories whose genesis and provenance accords remarkably well with economic theories from the same period (the mid 1970s and beyond), contemporary neuroscience, as the leading part of the new science of complexity, has pursued pathways which offer a challenge to the very fundamentals of Western science. Western science has long depended on the rigid separation of reason (logical deduction and empiricism) from affective bias (belief, superstition, 'gut' feelings). In the 1990s, however, neuroscientific research began to emerge in the public sphere which suggested that this historical division, which began with Descartes's dualism of mind and body in the seventeenth century, was an inaccurate picture of the way human knowing actually works. We might say that, while evolutionary theory still manifests elements of melancholic 'splitting' – Eldredge's opposing 'camps' in the evolutionary debate – neurobiology, in the melding of reason and emotion, offers us a truly mourningful science – interestingly, one that was foreshadowed in the 1930s by Tony Blair's favourite philosopher John Macmurray.

Gerald Edelman, in his 1992 book *Bright Air, Brilliant Fire: On the Matter of the Mind*, argues that mind arises out of the neural activity of the brain, which in turn is a response, at first, to the sensual experiences of the body.[36] Sensual experiences are registered neurologically. The body surfaces (senses) provide something like primitive 'maps' of experience which forge a counterpart in neuronal 'maps' in the brain. These 'maps' occur at many different sites in the brain but, extraordinarily, because most of the brain's networks spend more time speaking to each other than they do recording the sensual experiences provided by the body, the 'maps' are able to be integrated. This means that sensual experiences are experienced and retained in terms of memories, including their specific associations, and that the brain is able to call upon all these different maps in order to provide a complex supermap – which we call knowledge of the world. These 'memories' take the form of specific (that is to say individual) firings between different parts of the brain. They are 'hard-wired' inasmuch as particular parts of the brain will deal with them (although by no means in exactly the same way from individual to individual); but they are individual inasmuch as the particular associations (memories) will configure absolutely individual patterns of association. While particular parts of the body-brain will be involved in particular sorts of information-gathering, the ways in which neural and synaptic connections are formed will depend upon particular, individual, experiences. The brain, Edelman says, is not so much like a computational system as like a jungle. Each mind is like a complex eco-system: it must obey the laws of the world in which it finds itself (and we all share the same 'world' or eco-system), but each jungle develops according to the specific experiential sites upon which it grows. As Edelman says:

> ... although the connectivity of neuronal systems in the central nervous system (particularly those that are mapped) is more or less similar from individual to individual, it is not identical. Indeed ... there is considerable variation both in the shapes of individual neurons in a class and in their connection patterns. This is not surprising, given the stochastic (or statistically varying) nature of the developmental driving forces provided by cellular processes such as cell division, movement, and death [these are all observable processes during the development of multi-cellular development, organisation and life]; in some regions of the developing nervous system up to 70 percent of the neurons die before the structure of that region is completed! In general, therefore, uniquely specified connection cannot exist. If one were to number the branches of one neuron and to number in a corresponding manner the neurons it touched, the numbers would not correspond exactly in any two individuals of a species – not even in identical twins or in genetically identical animals.[37]

Edelman's insight – and his account of completing Darwin's project by providing an evolutionary explanation of mind – is to offer an evolutionary account of the development of neuronal maps; in these, on the basis of experience of the environment, some routes, or connections, between highways across the maps are re-enforced by repeated 'successes' and others are weakened. What counts as a successful set of connections is dictated by reinforcing responses from a very ancient part of the brain – the limbic system – situated at the base of the brain in the brain stem. The limbic system contains a number of evolutionarily selected 'values' which are good for survival. For example, eating is 'good', not eating is 'bad'; or grasping an object is 'good', not being able to grasp an object is 'bad'. To take the latter example (which was offered in a 1994 Horizon film on Edelman's work), an infant's attempts to reach out and grasp an object are initially random. When the infant manages to touch the object, the neuronal firings occurring at that moment in the cortex (the more recent, 'higher', part of the brain) are massively reinforced by floodings of 'positive' firings from the limbic system. (Think of the tremendous pleasure associated with the experience – whether physical or intellectual – of 'having got it!'.) These floodings reinforce the neuronal connections firing in the cortex at the moment of touching the object. With each repetition of 'success' (this is 'good'), particular routes, or connections, in the map are strengthened. Feelings, or urges from the limbic system, thus play a significant part in dictating what connections will be favoured for cortical mapping. The implications of this are far-reaching. Mind arises, as an effect of interactions with body/world, from complex interactions between different parts of the brain. For example, not only do all the different maps to do with seeing, touching – all the five senses in fact – interact with each other in forming neural maps, but the senses themselves are not dealt with only in one place in the brain. Seeing, for example, involves different parts of the brain interacting with each other. Some functions involved in seeing are not conscious; experiments have shown that we 'see' things – especially dangerous things – before we are conscious of seeing them. The amygdala (another very early part of the brain) sends out messages of 'danger' (such that heartbeat is raised, and adrenaline flows increase) *before* cortical recognition (consciousness of seeing something dangerous) has occurred.

Further, as I mentioned in the last chapter, research cited in Capra's *The Web of Life* indicates that it is wrong to think of the brain as only, or simply, in the skull. The work done by Candace Pert and her colleagues on peptides – molecular messengers – has shown that what were once thought of as three discrete systems – the nervous system, the endocrine system and the immune system – are all in fact one single psychosomatic network. Hormones, neurotransmitters, endorphins, and so on, all belong, it is now understood, to a single family of molecular messengers which, as Capra describes, are the biochemical manifestation of emotions; they play a crucial role in the co-ordinating activities of the immune system; they interlink and integrate mental, emotional, and biological activities. Peptides are not only produced and stored in the body, but in the brain also, leading Pert to say that she can 'no longer make a strong distinction between the brain and the body'.[38] Capra notes that, traditionally, neuroscientists have identified the limbic system with the production of emotions. This is correct: the limbic system is very rich in peptides. But this is not the only part of the body rich in peptide receptors: 'For example, the entire intestine is lined with peptide receptors. This is why we have "gut feelings". We literally feel our emotions in our gut'.[39] In other words, we are, more often than rationalists might like to suppose, creatures of instinct: instinct (evolved responses for success) crucially informs our rational or logical responses.

The modern (Enlightenment) cast of mind, which wishes to consider human behaviour in terms of logical, or calculable deductions and responses alone, is one which tries to ignore the animal basis of human being. But, in terms of evolutionary success, the attempt to reduce human beings to calculating, or calculable, machines is undoubtedly negative. Modernity's cult of the manager – who wishes to optimise efficiency – is, in terms of Darwinian neurobiology, a short cut to failure. In neo-Darwinian evolutionary biological terms, 'success' lies in allowing individuals to 'play', creatively, with their environment (this is how humans learn), or even to 'idle' while the brain talks creatively to itself. Here is Keats's state of diligent indolence – that slightly pleasant state of dreaminess in which one, nonetheless, attends: the limited courtier Consciousness waiting upon the magnificent and fascinatingly creative commands of the monarch Mind. In order to be truly efficient, we need to make room for behaviour which, on the surface and 'logically' will often seem inefficient. In other words, 'real efficiency' (i.e. making creative progress) will often (from a manager's point of view) look like time wasting. What is most creative (and, in evolutionary terms, successful) in human behaviour will, from a manager's point of view, look inefficient and unproductive. The problem is that the manager is driven by an emaciated rationalist and short-term view of efficiency. What may end up being truly efficient is letting people play – and play is endlessly creative and essentially incalculable.

The model emerging from the field of neuroscience suggests that there is a remarkable degree of plasticity in the neural networks of the brain – and thus in associative ideas and mental representations – and that, amongst other things, our sense of belonging (to a particular community of relatedness) is as much a question of cultural representation and identification as of simple genetics. In this sense, it is worth remembering that *all* human beings are very closely genetically related. In principle there is as much reason to define my 'family' in terms of the whole human race as there is to see it as small, and limited to those I know. What we call a society is a complex set of learned relationships and attendant ideas (or conscious and unconscious representations). Freud's attention to our powerful early relationships is shown to be doubly right in the light of neurobiology's story of neural mapping. These early relationships (neural maps deeply inscribed by the affects) must become the *affectively* analogical models for later experiences. Clearly, they are not the only ones (remember the extraordinary number and complexity of relations between synapses); millions upon millions of other significant experiences and ideas are always also potentially in play in the mind's extraordinarily complex interaction with the world. The brain is a constantly active living system of systems, which works in a way which must be (can *only* be) akin to language, using analogy, association, similarity and dissimilarity, narrative, metaphor and metonymy.[40] One might even suspect that the great symbols that exist in our cultural life, around which the affective accretions of time collect, correspond to the powerful flows of the emotions in the brain which inform everything we do.

It has been pointed out that social Darwinist explanations of human behaviour gain credence during periods when economic theories of *laissez faire* are dominant – during the 1880s and 1890s, and during the 1980s and 1990s, for example. Richard Dawkins's 'selfish gene' appeared at the same time as neo-liberalism's rationalist insistence on utilitarian theories of self-interested individualism. Mounting a challenge to all of this from the side of human complexity, plasticity, and non-rationalist accounting, neuroscientific accounts of human reason introduce an anti-cartesian view of human beings, in which mind and body are in a constant state of complex interaction, and in which mind is embodied and body enworlded. To be a human being is to be part of a vast, complex, interacting, feedback-looping system. Readers may recall my earlier references to the philosophy of Leibniz as launching an organicist and anti-cartesian view of the relationship between individual and whole, from which romanticism would, eventually, draw some of its most interesting insights: ('monads ... are dynamic and evolving, but there is a relationship between each individual monad and the universe which is indissoluble ... each individual [monad] expresses the universe from a particular viewpoint'). As Coveney and Highfield point out, Leibniz's invention of the calculus (more or less at the same time as Newton) formed part of the attempt to put forward an ambitious scheme to formalise all human thought and mathematics into a universal language.[41] This 'visionary' work was, they note, part of the quest continued by the pioneers of artificial intelligence 300 years later. In other words, from Leibniz to complexity theory we come full circle, through the *longeurs* of the oppositions described by Raymond Williams in *Culture and Society*, to something like an *artistic* science: the search for 'unity from diversity' can be found as much in contemporary science as in Coleridge's *Biographia Literaria*. In contrast to all this, the work of geneticists like Richard Dawkins has led more or less directly, at the popular level, to an essentially neoconservative and Hobbesian view of human behaviour – much as they might dislike this. The implication of these theories *for some* is that, if you wish to make the world a better place, you must understand the crude logic of genetic survival.

Complexity theory, in all the variations and symptomatic manifestations alluded to here, seems to open the door once closed by modernity between science, art and religion. Perhaps we had to close that door for a time for good reasons. But now we are opening it again for equally good reasons, because we are beginning to understand that these apparently different aspects of our lives are not, in fact, strictly separable. Coveney and Highfield talk, for example, about 'the religion of mathematics' and the 'artist's code'. Mathematics, it turns out, cannot always provide us with internally consistent theories which also contain their own proof. The work of the mathematician Kurt Gödel unnervingly demonstrated that Aristotle's Law of the Excluded Middle is false because there will always be statements, even in arithmetic, whose truth value is undecidable 'without using methods from outside the logical system in question':

> In effect, Gödel showed the inevitability of finding logical paradoxes in arithmetic that are the equivalent of the statement 'this sentence is false'.
>
> To make matters worse, he also showed that it is never possible to prove that a mathematical system is itself logically self-consistent. One must always step outside a formal mathematical calculus to determine its validity.[42]

Coveney and Highfield go on to quote John Barrow: 'If we define a religion to be a system of thought which contains unprovable statements, so it contains an element of faith, then Gödel has taught us that not only is mathematics a religion but it is the only religion able to prove itself to be one.'

CONCLUSIONS

What, then, are the implications of this understanding of body-mind – and must it be, as some people might fear, necessarily conservative or anti-progressive, in order to respond to obscure feelings about things? Clearly, responding to feelings is what normal human beings do most of the time. As John Macmurray pointed out sixty years ago, our rationalisations for actions are often simply about giving the *appearance* of rationality to actions not intrinsically rational (in the 'old' sense of reason as free of affect) at all.[43] The question then arises of what it might mean to *acknowledge* that we are embodied and enworlded creatures who respond affectively to the world when we reason? And what are the implications of thinking of human societies as complex non-linear systems (sometimes giving rise to chaotic behaviours), in which (in Leibnizian and Edelmanist fashion) each individual is an absolutely unique expression of the evolved totality of the whole at the time of its existence?

One sort of answer to these questions may be found in the kinds of work – described at the beginning of this chapter – being undertaken by institutions such as the New Economics Foundation, The Relationships Foundation and Antidote. Here, how we feel about our world – whether in terms of our human or non-human environment – is being taken, literally, into account. But what of politics and the law which, since Bentham's day, have increasingly aimed at rationality based on the hard data of statistics and empirical research? Perhaps here the effect might be a sort a negative benefit, in which researchers and policy-makers are obliged to acknowledge a dimension which cannot be directly revealed by such means. Taking emotion into account might make life (and policy-making) more complex, but it will undoubtedly make it more human. Emotional and social auditing of the kind described by James Park of Antidote is likely, for instance, to reveal much more complex causes of, say, teenage single motherhood, or long-term unemployment, than do assumptions which stop at 'access to housing or benefits', or thinking of people as being generally feckless and workshy.

What contemporary neuroscience tells us is that the separation of 'cool' rationality from 'warm' feelings is neurologically speaking a fiction. Edelman's work on the biology of the brain and the nature of mind indicates that the rationalist's determination to exclude feelings and hunches as irrational is likely to be, eventually, counter-productive from an evolutionary point of view. This view is also supported by Antonio Damasio's work on the effects of physical damage on those parts of the brain involved in transmitting values, evolved early in the life of the species because they proved to be of evolutionary value.[44]

The historical Enlightenment commitment to rationality conceived of as the pursuit of calculation and the suppression of illogical feelings and impulses leads to a second problem: the nature of the kinds of human beings likely to be produced by child-rearing practices which are based upon 'rational' practices alone. I raised this problem in Chapter 2; and as I said there, a child who is insufficiently 'held', and whose affective life is ignored, is likely to lack the forms of emotional identification (practical love) which enable it to have a fully responsive (and responsible) internal world. Readers will remember that I commented on the rise, over the twentieth century, of what have become known as borderline personalities – individuals whose internal worlds are lacking in affective structures. Edelman's book is dedicated to Darwin and to Freud, and it is easy to see how, as both Edelman and Damasio remark, the Freudian account of the mapping of the affective world – especially as that is elaborated by Object Relations analysts such as Melanie Klein and Donald Winnicott – can very easily be transposed into neurobiological terms. As Damasio's laboratory research with brain damaged individuals indicates, the capacity to reason can remain intact, but where certain kinds of choices are concerned (e.g. prioritising in work or social situations and making choices from a range of possibilities), if there is damage to areas concerned with the transmission of feelings (such as hunches or intuitions based upon a lifetime's experience and engraved in our neural maps but not accessible to consciousness), then patients consistently make extremely poor, normal-life-destroying choices.[45] For those who have wished to write off Freudian insights, it is worth emphasising that Freud's early 'Project for a Scientific Psychology', which sought to locate mind in the chemistry of the brain, *and* his later insights concerning the role of fantasy and affect (psychical representations) in the construction of reality, are, if sometimes necessarily crude or tentative, largely vindicated by recent developments in neuroscience. Freud helped us to begin to tell a story (upon which this whole book is predicated) in which world, body and mind are, *together*, wholly implicated in the kinds of stories we can tell, and in the possible evolution of better stories and better worlds.

Feelings inform everything we do and are central to our evolutionary success. But we learn what to do with feelings from our experiences in the world. Where our life experiences have been in some way abnormal or disturbed, especially in infancy and childhood, our affective neural maps will be absent, partial or disordered. Freud's description of the topography of the mind, filled with chains of overdetermined associations between words, events and conscious and unconscious memories, which describe particular pathways etched by the affects cathected to them in our psychical life, is remarkably close to the neurobiologists' description of neural mapping, especially in infancy and childhood, as being engraved by powerful flows of feeling.

The strength of contemporary neuroscientific theories lies, it seems to me, in the ways in which these put back our affective enworlded bodies into an understanding of human reason. The science is still Darwinian, but it offers an account of evolution able to remind harsher proponents of Darwinism that there is much more to human life than icy competition and rational calculation of self-interest. Human beings have survived because they are creatures whose passions, however violent, matter.

Rationality, logic and empiricism have provided us with many advantages in our struggle to survive, but, inasmuch as these have been over-valued, and the affective life which underpins them undervalued and seen as inimical to reason, they have encouraged and given succour to views of life which, when really understood, are actually intolerable for most human beings. That this is so may go some way to explain the emergence of various kinds of romanticism, including the most recent New Age versions, but these resistances to the harshness of utilitarianism – which is essentially a philosophy of effectiveness and managerialism – speak to a truth now being uncovered by the rational pursuit of scientific method itself.

As Damasio's research points out, our affective lives matter, and when they are disabled – whether by physical trauma, emotionally illiterate upbringing, or by wider ideological values – we become less human and more like the 'pods' and 'replicants' of the post-war 'scientific imagination'. Michael Schluter and David Lee's *The R Factor*, which stresses the importance of human relations and of relational proximity in our social lives as workers and politically autonomous individuals, can be thought of as a practical application of theoretical neuroscience. This is, similarly, the case with Daniel Goleman's *Emotional Intelligence*, which explores the effects of affective adequacy and inadequacy. Goleman discusses psychopaths (more recently termed sociopaths) as well-known examples of some form of affective failure, and, in particular, as failures in empathic identification: often charming but cold and remorseless, unable to feel empathy or compassion and unable to make true emotional connections with other people. Goleman goes on to point out that some researchers suspect that some instances of psychopathy may be related to a neural defect; some laboratory experiments have indicated that the brain responses of psychopaths do not show the normal distinctive responses to certain stimuli:

> A possible physiological basis of heartless psychopathy has been shown in two ways, both of which suggest the involvement of neural pathways to the limbic brain. In one, people's brainwaves are measured as they try to decipher words that have been scrambled. The words are flashed very quickly, for just a tenth of a second or so. Most people react differently to emotional words such as *kill* than to neutral words such a *chair*; they can decide more quickly if the emotional word was scrambled, and their brains show a distinctive wave pattern in response to the emotional words, but not the neutral ones. But psychopaths have neither of these responses; their brains do not show the distinctive pattern in response to the emotional words, and they do not respond more quickly to them, suggesting a disruption in circuits between the verbal cortex, which recognises the word, and the limbic brain which attaches feeling to it.[46]

Goleman does not reference Edelman's work, although he does reference Damasio, but we know from the former that the neuronal circuits – or what Edelman calls neuronal 'maps' – are laid down in response to environmental experience. It may well be that some forms of psychopathy are caused by congenital defects in the brain, but it seems just as likely that psychopaths suffer from the creation, through reinforced early experiences, of deviant mapping. Once again, we are in the sphere of infant and child care and the (intended or unintended) results of what Goleman describes as emotional education. In its discussion of 'as if's' and False Selves, psycho-analysis, as discussed in earlier chapters, has also had much of interest to say in this regard.

Contemporary developments in complexity theory and evolutionary biology are, in my view, potentially politically important. Not only are the books I have referred to here part of an increasing interest in popular science, but they also indicate a significant shift in the ways in which evolutionary science is producing a radically new, post-Enlightenment account of what it means to be human. It is not the case that we are likely ever to go beyond the 'universal acid' of what Dennett called 'Darwin's dangerous idea', but it *is* the case that the dangerous idea is being explored in ways that may make Darwinism less frightening and less corrosive. A world which could both understand the importance of the emotions, and the creativity and 'hunch-like' nature of human reasoning, and see the human as a complex being interacting within larger complex systems, would be a far kinder and more interesting world than that imagined and promoted by utilitarianism's ice-cold and inhuman rationality.

In *The Emotional Brain*, Joseph LeDoux, like Edelman, considers that psychoanalytic practice enacts something like an emotional 're-mapping'. Both agree that the process of psychoanalysis requires a great deal of time because the pathway from the evolutionarily ancient amygdala to the more recent frontal cortex overshadows the pathway from the cortex to the amygdala. In other words, emotional input into conscious reasoning is stronger than the input of consciousness into emotional responses; a great deal of time and work, conscious and unconscious, is required to alter neuronal maps engrained with feelings: the relatively recent advantages of conscious thought are weak compared with the deeply established benefits of having a speedy emotional response to stimuli. Freud's insight about the central, and practical, importance of the Transference in the success of the therapeutic relationship is underlined by neurobiology. The Transference, or as Freud also called it 'transference love', is essential to psychical remaking because the connections in our brain-minds are *emotionally* engraved.

Considering the relatively recent evolutionary development of the cortex, LeDoux suggests that, since 'the cortical connections with the amygdala are far greater in primates than in other mammals', we might be right to conclude that 'these connections continue to expand' and that 'the cortex might gain more and more control over the amygdala, possibly allowing future humans to be better able to control their emotions'.[47] Further, and more importantly,

> The increased connectivity between the amygdala and the cortex
> involves fibers going from the cortex to the amygdala as well as from

the amygdala to the cortex. If these nerve pathways strike a balance, it is possible that the struggle between thought and emotion may ultimately be resolved not by the dominance of emotional centers by cortical cognitions, but by a more harmonious integration of reason and passion. With increased connectivity between the cortex and the amygdala, cognition and emotion might begin to work together rather than separately ... But wouldn't it be wonderful if we did understand where our emotions were taking us from moment to moment, day to day, and year to year, and why? If the trends toward cognitive-emotional connectivity in the brain are any indication, our brains may, in fact, be moving in this direction.[48]

In other words, one could suggest that, if these developments in neurobiological understanding take practical root in our self-understandings in the world, and if we begin to understand the advantage of taking proper account of our feelings about things, we may well be paving the way for selection on the basis of adaptation to environment, to increase the numbers of human beings who are careful with feelings. Against the historical legacy of an over-emphasis upon counter-intuitive rationality which I discussed in Chapter 2, such new understandings and developments would be a prize worth having.

It seems to me that Enlightenment modernity, with its emphasis on rationality at the expense of emotions, has proved detrimental to our ability to empathise with other human creatures, and thus has tended to produce generations of individuals whose actions are inimical to the development of wholesome, integrated human beings. The new insights of neurobiology attest to the symptomatic emergence of an historical corrective to this trend. We once had religion to bind together (not without cost) our affective needs and our reason; then science stepped in and declared war on everything beyond logic, reason and empirical proof. Now it seems that sections of the scientific community have begun to see the folly of this approach and are turning us back to what, in an earlier mode, scientists thought they should exclude. In allowing us to rethink ourselves as richly obscure affective creatures who are what we are because we are absolutely embedded in the natural and social worlds, contemporary neuroscience offers to restore us not only to evolutionary success but to a more humanly decent way of being in the world. The old Enlightenment is truly over. The new modernity has begun.

NOTES

1 See C.P. Snow, *The Two Cultures*, Introduction by Stefan Collini, Cambridge University Press, Cambridge 1993. Collini's Introduction is particularly helpful in providing history and context.

2 D. Cupitt, *After God: the Future of Religion*, Weidenfeld & Nicolson, London 1997, p92.

3 See M. Klein, 'Mourning and Its Relation to Manic-Depressive States', in J. Mitchell (ed), *The Selected Melanie Klein*, Penguin, Harmondsworth 1986.

4 W. Wheeler, 'After Grief? What Kinds of Inhuman Selves?', *New Formations*, 25, Summer 1995.

5 K. Davey, 'Anxiety and Identification on the British Left', in Anne Coddington & M. Perryman (eds), *The Moderniser's Dilemma: Radical Politics in the Age of Blair*, Lawrence & Wishart, London 1998, p275.

6 See Paul Boghossian's discussion of this in relation to the *Social Text* hoax (note 7 following) in P. Boghossian, 'What the Sokal hoax ought to teach us', *Times Literary Supplement*, 13 December 1996.

7 A. Sokal, 'Transgressing the Boundaries: towards a transformative hermeneutics of quantum gravity', *Social Text*, vol. 14, no. 46/7, (Spring/Summer 1996).

8 S.J. Gould, *Wonderful Life*, Penguin, Harmondsworth 1991, p51.

9 R. Dawkins, *The Selfish Gene*, Oxford University Press, Oxford, 1989[1976].

10 *Ibid.*, p199.

11 *Ibid.*, pp200-1.

12 N. Eldredge, *Reinventing Darwin: The Great Evolutionary Debate*, Phoenix, London 1996, px.

13 F. Capra, *The Web of Life: A New Synthesis of Mind and Matter*, HarperCollins, London 1996, p222.

14 D. Cupitt, 1997, *op. cit.*, p66.

15 G. Edelman, *Bright Air, Brilliant Fire: On the Matter of Mind*, Penguin, Harmondsworth 1994, p68.

16 *Ibid.*, p233.

17 K. Devlin, *Goodbye, Descartes: The End of Logic and the Search for a New Cosmology of the Mind*, John Wiley, Chichester 1997.

18 T. Adorno, *Minima Moralia: Reflections from Damaged Life*, tr. E.F.N. Jephcott, Verso, London 1974, p15.

19 J. Habermas, 'Modernity versus Postmodernity', *New German Critique*, 22, Winter 1981.

20 P. Coveney & R. Highfield, *Frontiers of Complexity: The Search for Order*

in a Chaotic World, Faber & Faber, London 1995, p7.

21 *Ibid.*.

22 *Ibid.*, p10.

23 *Ibid.*, p8.

24 *Ibid.*, p13.

25 *Ibid.*, p14.

26 *Ibid.*, p11.

27 Some kinds of economic theory seem utterly impenetrable. I offer G.J. Deboeck's (ed) *Trading on the Edge: Neural, Genetic, and Fuzzy Systems for Chaotic Financial Markets*, John Wiley, Chichester, 1994, as an example of the genre of economists who use complexity theory. I am not in a position to judge its value.

28 P. Heelas, *The New Age Movement*, Blackwell, Oxford 1996, p66.

29 See Schluter's book on relational matrices, especially as these effect economics, M. Schluter and D. Lee, *The R Factor*, Hodder & Stoughton, London 1993.

30 J. Park, from text of Nexus 'Third Way' Conference paper supplied by the author.

31 M. Ridley, *The Origins of Virtue*, Viking, Harmondsworth 1996, pp131-2.

32 *Ibid.*, p136

33 Frank, cited in *ibid.*, p141.

34 *Ibid.*, p143.

36 Edelman, 1994, *op. cit.*.

37 *Ibid.*, p25.

38 Cited in Capra, 1996, *op. cit.*, p276.

39 *Ibid.*, p277.

40 I have subsequently found some support for this view in an on-line journal called *Neuroscience Update* (1995) in which Robert P. Pula writes: 'I wrote in 1970, "That language structures reflect neural structures and, by feedback mechanisms, may ALTER neural structures, is one of the eminently plausible speculations of Korzybski in support of which we have, as yet, insufficient data". Much of what follows in Edelman's book provides additional support for what Korzybski was writing from the 1920s through 1950.'

41 Coveney & Highfield, 1995, *op. cit.*, p22.

42 *Ibid.*, p28.

43 J. Macmurray, *Reason and Emotion*, Faber & Faber, London 1995, pp11-14.

44 A Damasio, *Descartes's Error: Emotion, Reason and the Human Brain*, Picador, London 1994.

45 For a fuller account, see 'A Modern Phineas Cage', in Damasio, *op. cit.*, p34 *ff*.

46 D. Goleman, *Emotional Intelligence: Why it Can Matter More than IQ*, Bloomsbury, London 1996, p109.
47 J. LeDoux, *The Emotional Brain: The Mysterious Underpinnings of Emotional Life*, Weidenfeld & Nicolson, London 1998, p303.
48 *Ibid.*

More lenient myths

The predictions for life in Britain up to the year 2020 in the Henley Centre's *NeXt Generation: Lifestyles for the future* (1998) make fairly disturbing reading. Out of its four generational groups – 'Senior' (born between 1930 and 1945), 'Baby Boomers' (1946 to 1961), 'Generation Xers' (1962 to 1977), and 'Millennium Kids' (1978 to 1993) – the Seniors are the last generation to have any experience of significant stability. For the rest the future is likely to consist of temporary contract work (some of it from home), serial monogamy, and late single parenthood:

> Life will be a series of negotiations and trade-offs ... The end of the 'job for life' or 'partner for life' means time spent making new choices and renewing contracts ... In a world of choice, there will always be less popular options. These options may actually be people, who will become outcasts if they cannot stand the pace of change or cannot be self-sufficient.[1]

At present, both Generation Xers and Millennium Kids appear to be apathetic about, or uninterested in, traditional party politics, believing that: 'It doesn't make any difference [whether we vote], at the end of the day we don't get what we want'. The Henley report cites a City University report – 'Twentysomethings in the 1990s' – as recording 'In a recent survey of 28 year olds, only 40 per cent believed that political parties could do anything to benefit them, whilst 44 per cent reckoned that "Politicians are mainly in politics for their own benefit and not for the benefit of the community"'.[2] The report also records the increasing fragmentation of traditional ties – 'Family, geography – the communities of coincidence and history are dwindling. Instead we're seeing more changing liaisons, whether they are virtual or real, shifting and changing like mad'[3] – and suggests (what is already evident today) a tendency to look to quasi-religious or mystical sources for condolence. The picture presented by the Henley Report is thus a deeply pessimistic one, characterised by increasing fragmentation in the two areas in which people have tended to find a sense of identity: work and family home.

However, I can see a more optimistic route open to us. As I have argued in this book, the signs of our times can be read as evidence of what I have called mourning which, unlike cultural melancholia, is a positive and ultimately a healthy response to loss. Much of the intellectual and creative work done during the past decade or so can be characterised in this way. Loss of any treasured thing – and particularly of 'big' things like certainty, tradition, and God – is profoundly traumatising. The melancholic's response is a refusal to let go, in which the lost object is 'kept' through internalisation, but also punished for going away. Melancholia is, thus, characterised by punitive and vicious self-loathing, and by an inability to let go and move on. The mourner on the other hand, although always utterly transformed by the loss of what was once held dear and depended upon, is able to transform the shattered fragments of an earlier self and world, and to build something new from those fragments and ruins. Doing this involves a radical reformulation – a resymbolisation – of experience, so that old and familiar ways of understanding things are reconfigured, and old certainties and values understood in quite different ways. This is, I have suggested, what has been happening over the past quarter of a century. The old cartesian divide is in the process of giving way to more complex holistic models of both the individual's understanding of the relationship between mind and body and, more widely, the relationship between individual creatures and the living world of which they are a living part. I have not found space to talk about the development of ecological ideas since the 1970s but, pressed for a phrase to describe the sensibility which underlies all these changes generally, 'ecological sensibility' is the one I would choose.

The Henley Centre Report on the future seems to be firmly predicated on the kind of future we will have if the present condition of the global dominance of free market capitalism continues. As very many people have pointed out, capitalism is inherently unstable and it destabilises everything it touches. Sometimes this is very good for human ingenuity but, as has also been said many times, it does not seem to be very good for human happiness. Having thought, a decade ago, that the left vastly underrated both the power and pleasure of consumption,[4] I now wonder whether the consuming passions party hasn't turned into something like an orgy in the last days of Rome. Commodification, marketisation and contractualism seem to invade every area of human life. Melanie Klein tells the story of a woman (actually Klein herself) in an acute state of melancholic grieving for whom even the light of the sun seemed artificial and unreal. A commodified world lit by a neon sun seems a good way of describing the world which global capital seems to want to make. Yet, as I hope I have managed to show, there *are* ways in which such a grimness can be, and is being, resisted. Understanding the nature of human minds and their absolute intimacy with the bodies and world through which they are made may help us to understand that what goes on in the world *is* our mind. Thomas Carlyle was closer to the truth than he could ever have imagined when he worried about modernity's mechanisation of the head as well as the hand. The assaults we experience upon our senses – whether directly or via the extensions of our global media – are literally assaults upon our souls; and, like all vicious things, they wound and deform. Conforming to a brutal world in which ugliness and greed are considered (by so-called 'realists') to be inevitable, or even desirable for the most robustly competitive markets, is to assent to an assault on one's very humanity. Cohesive societies constitute virtuous circles because they make cohesive minds. As Paul Ormerod concludes in *The Death of Economics*, societies and economies are not neatly made up of rational economic individuals, they are complex non-linear systems which react in highly complex ways. Full-employment and social cohesion, he argues, are achievable aims once we shake off the myth that the free market is incompatible with some kind of code of collective responsibilities:

> The name of Adam Smith is regularly invoked by those who subscribe to this latter concept.
> But Adam Smith was a philosopher as well as an economist, famous in his time as much for his *Theory of the Moral Sentiments* as for *The Wealth of Nations*. And as he understood so well, society *is* more than the sum of its individual parts.[5]

Ormerod's economic view of economies and societies as complex, non-linear, systems is what I would call ecological. Social cohesion, a holistic and ecological view of ourselves and our relationship to the world which makes us, and human creativity, are all things which are antagonistic to commodification. There *is* such a thing as society, and there *is* an alternative to free market competition run amok.

Such a society might look a little like European social democracy, but radically informed by a new ecology of mind and environment and politics in which what counts as human profit is redefined according to a more subtle understanding of 'all souls'. 'Hard' evolutionists such as Matt Ridley would say that, while we may be genetically programmed to favour altruism in others as a sign of cooperativeness, our individual behaviour is largely selfish, and it is only when we have a material stake in co-operating that our better impulses come to the fore because then the benefits of reciprocity are evident. Ridley's answer is 'devolution', so that 'social and material exchange' amongst groups small enough to appreciate the benefits of reciprocity are able to re-establish the trust which is also a part of our evolutionary make-up, and is 'the foundation of virtue'. When we join together the arguments of the geneticists with the arguments of the evolutionary neurobiologists, and think about their place alongside similar lines of thought in literature and philosophy, economics and management theory, we can see the beginnings of ideas which might eventually improve the world we live in. The old hopes of the philosophers of the first Enlightenment – that the application of human reason would lay the foundations of a better world – may be better realised in these new ideas, now most helpfully underpinned by new scientific understandings, which argue that human feelings are a *part* of human reason, not its undoing. We would do well to understand our self-consciousness as an intimate *being* in a world in which both self and other, subject and object, are in a gradual state of reciprocal revelation. Reciprocating communities, more conscious of human affect and of the consequences of various forms of environmental violence, might be good things to aim for.

I am not making a case for the 'perfectibility' of humankind, I am simply suggesting that a fuller, more whole and more holistic understanding of ourselves and the way we connect with others is possible. The goal of human solidarity and community is a hopeful one but it is one that can only be forged – as in Graham Swift's community of Bermondsey friends who do the work of mourning in *Last Orders* – in local ways. Globalisation is probably one of our greatest problems as the twenty-first century gets underway. The other is the great extremes of inequality in access to materials and power. A more ecological sensibility, in all the senses in which I have discussed it here, might help us to begin to think about ways in which greed can be constrained so that the benefits of reciprocity can be made clearer for all concerned. Clearly, this will take a great deal of political courage and creative ingenuity. The building of a new modernity will be a long and difficult task, but we do now have some of the forms of knowledge – about how human beings are, and about how our better inheritances can be encouraged – which might allow us to work, *together*, towards this goal. At the end of a 300 year long attempt to disenchant the world, we slowly come to recognise that we are the world and the world is us, and life is a constant process of creative interchange between body and soul. To paraphrase Graham Swift's 'new realism': mourning will become us when we realise that this complex reciprocity is, indeed, what we're made of.

NOTES

1   *NeXt Generation*: *Lifestyles for the future*, The Henley Centre, London 1998, p6.
2   *Ibid.*, pp32 and 33.
3   *Ibid.*, p17.
4   See, for example, B. Campbell & W. Wheeler, 'Filofaxions', *Marxism Today*, December 1988.
5   P. Ormerod, *The Death of Economics*, Faber & Faber, London 1994, p212.
6   Ridley, *The Origins of Virtue*, Viking, Harmondsworth 1996, p265.

Index